Conceptual Foundations of Teaching Reading

SOLVING PROBLEMS IN THE TEACHING OF LITERACY

Cathy Collins Block, *Series Editor*

Recent Volumes

EXPLAINING READING: A RESOURCE FOR TEACHING
CONCEPTS, SKILLS, AND STRATEGIES
Gerald G. Duffy

RETHINKING READING COMPREHENSION
Edited by Anne P. Sweet and Catherine E. Snow

EXEMPLARY LITERACY TEACHERS: PROMOTING SUCCESS
FOR ALL CHILDREN IN GRADES K–5
Cathy Collins Block and John N. Mangieri

ASSESSMENT FOR READING INSTRUCTION
Michael C. McKenna and Steven A. Stahl

VOCABULARY INSTRUCTION: RESEARCH TO PRACTICE
Edited by James F. Baumann and Edward J. Kame'enui

THE READING SPECIALIST: LEADERSHIP FOR THE CLASSROOM,
SCHOOL, AND COMMUNITY
Rita M. Bean

MULTICULTURAL AND MULTILINGUAL LITERACY AND LANGUAGE:
CONTEXTS AND PRACTICES
Edited by Fenice B. Boyd and Cynthia H. Brock, with Mary S. Rozendal

TEACHING ALL THE CHILDREN:
STRATEGIES FOR DEVELOPING LITERACY IN AN URBAN SETTING
Edited by Diane Lapp, Cathy Collins Block, Eric J. Cooper,
James Flood, Nancy Roser, and Josefina Villamil Tinajero

CONCEPTUAL FOUNDATIONS OF TEACHING READING
Mark Sadoski

Conceptual Foundations of Teaching Reading

MARK SADOSKI

THE GUILFORD PRESS
NEW YORK LONDON

© 2004 The Guilford Press
A Division of Guilford Publications, Inc.
72 Spring Street, New York, NY 10012
www.guilford.com

This book is printed on acid-free paper.

Last digit is print number: 9   8   7   6   5   4   3   2   1

Library of Congress Cataloging-in-Publication Data

Sadoski, Mark.
 Conceptual foundations of teaching reading / Mark Sadoski.
   p. cm. — (Solving problems in the teaching of literacy)
 Includes bibliographical references and index.
 ISBN 1-59385-036-0 (pbk.) — ISBN 1-59385-037-9 (hard cover)
 1. Reading. 2. Curriculum planning. I. Title. II. Series.
 LB1050.S135 2004
 418.4´019—dc22   2003027497

For Carol

About the Author

Mark Sadoski, PhD, is a Professor and Distinguished Research Fellow in the College of Education and Human Development at Texas A&M University. He holds joint appointments in the Department of Teaching, Learning, and Culture, and the Department of Educational Psychology. He was a classroom teacher and reading clinician in the public schools for 13 years, serving K–12 and adult education, before entering academia full-time. He has published widely in top literacy journals for more than 20 years, and he serves on the editorial boards of *Reading Research Quarterly, Journal of Literacy Research, Reading Psychology,* and *Reading and Writing.* He is also coauthor of the theoretical book *Imagery and Text: A Dual Coding Theory of Reading and Writing* (2001). Dr. Sadoski speaks widely at professional conferences and as a private consultant. His professional interests include curriculum, instruction, and assessment in classroom and clinic, and the psychology of literacy.

Preface and Acknowledgments

The biggest challenge facing the student of reading education is how to sort it all out. The field is burdened with conflicting conceptualizations, approaches, and methods, and all their attendant jargon. Each generation seems to add new methods and approaches as new discoveries are made and as earlier approaches are revised or renamed. Efforts to codify and taxonomize our knowledge of the teaching of reading are rudimentary compared to the taxonomic systems that have been developed in many other fields. Proposed systems have tended to be either too simple or too complex, and they have often been the product of academic rationalism, untested with practitioners in the field.

This book is an effort to address the organizational problems of those learning the principles and practices of teaching reading and to incrementally advance the effort to bring conceptual order to the field, with emphasis on the first purpose. It is intended for students preparing for careers in teaching, inservice teachers, alternative or postbaccalaureate students, educational administration students, psychology or educational psychology students, and even the involved parent or policymaker interested in the teaching of reading. The principles elaborated here can serve as the basis for policy and curriculum planning as well as instructional design and delivery.

The book attempts to keep the definitions of terms consistent with those in *The Literacy Dictionary* (Harris & Hodges, 1995), a standard reference in the field. Efforts to codify the knowledge and nomenclature of the field deserve mutual support. However, some terms used here may deviate from definitions included there. Where this is the case, special attention is paid to explanation. Some terms such as *method* and *approach* are very general, are not defined in *The Literacy Dictionary*, and are used in a very general sense here. The term *approach* is perhaps the broader term, but in the field the two terms are used almost interchangeably.

This book began in 1980 when Professor William D. Page handed me the final report of a federally sponsored empirical study of the theoretical bases of reading programs and encouraged me to "do something with this." Bill Page was an encouraging force behind many ambitious projects (e.g., George Hillocks's [1986] taxonomic review and meta-analysis of the field of teaching writing). This invitation eventually led me to read or reread the research of Gray, Chall, Corder, Downing, and other scholars who had attempted to bring order to the knowledge base of teaching reading. This in turn led me to develop and test a simplified and practical conceptual framework for the teaching of reading with the help of my students at Southern Connecticut State University and Texas A&M University (Sadoski, 1982). This book is a summarized and updated version of that system, which became a series of lectures in my classes over the years. Therefore, the first acknowledgments are due to Bill Page, who passed on nearly 20 years ago, and to my students, who inherited his spirit of inquiry.

The book is lovingly dedicated to my wife, Carol, who helps more than she knows in reading drafts, commenting, and generally being supportive. Her forbearance with my bookishness is most appreciated.

Figure 2.2 is from an edition of the *New England Primer* published by Benjamin Olds in 1826. Figure 2.3 is from an edition of Noah Webster's *American Spelling Book* published by Holbrook and Fessenden in 1824. Both figures were reproduced through the courtesy of the Department of Special Collections, Kenneth Spencer Research Library, University of Kansas. The generous assistance of Richard W. Clement, Special Collections Librarian, is gratefully acknowledged. Permission to reproduce Figure 2.4 from an 1879 edition of the McGuffey reader was provided by John Wiley & Sons. The text and illustrations in Figure 2.5 are from page 34 in *We Look and See*, copyright 1951 by Scott, Foresman and Company, and are reprinted by permission of Pearson Education, Inc. The figures in Chapters 4, 5, and 6 were produced by Molly Scopel at Texas A&M University. Figure 7.1 is printed with the permission of Tom Sadoski. Figure 8.1 is from the National Center for Educational Statistics, U.S. Department of Education. Figure 8.2 is copyrighted by the International Reading Association, and is reprinted with permission of Michael C. McKenna and the International Reading Association. All rights reserved. I extend my personal thanks to all those mentioned above, as well as to Chris Jennison, Senior Editor at The Guilford Press, for his knowledgeable and courteous assistance in all phases of this book.

MARK SADOSKI
College Station, Texas

REFERENCES

Harris, T. L., & Hodges, R. E. (1995). *The literacy dictionary: The vocabulary of reading and writing.* Newark, DE: International Reading Association.

Hillocks, G. Jr. (1986). *Research on written composition: New directions for teaching.* Urbana, IL: ERIC Clearinghouse on Reading and Communication Skills and the National Conference on Research in English.

Sadoski, M. (1982). *A study of the theoretical bases of reading instruction and a comparison of programs.* Texas A&M University Instructional Research Laboratory Technical Paper No. R83001. (ERIC Document Reproduction Service No. ED 236 543)

Contents

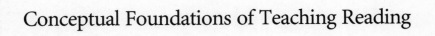

Conceptual Foundations of Teaching Reading

CHAPTER 1

Introduction, Background, and Structure of This Book

This book was written for three primary purposes:

- For beginners, to provide a framework for understanding the teaching of reading that will organize much of their subsequent learning.
- For more advanced students, to provide a system for bringing order to the confusion of undifferentiated concepts that often accompanies learning about the teaching of reading.
- For scholars and theorists of reading, to incrementally advance the effort to bring conceptual order to the knowledge base for teaching reading.

The teaching of reading, especially elementary reading, is one of the most debated subjects in education and even among the general public. Like religion and politics, it seems to kindle contention even among the mild-mannered. Perhaps this is because we value our children so much, for ensuring children the opportunities that the ability to read affords is a value deeply ingrained in our society. It befits any teacher, administrator, concerned parent, or policy-maker to have a clear and organized understanding of this most basic subject.

However, even introductory books on the subject of teaching reading too often become immediately enmeshed in conflicting details of method, approach, and theory. This poses a perplexing problem for the beginning educator trying to establish a firm base on which to build. Even graduate students in education are often perplexed by the conceptual congestion and tangled terminology of the subject. And well they might be, for fully understanding reading and its teaching involves ideas from psychology, linguistics, sociology, anthropology, education, literary studies, technology, and many other areas. Few fields are more multifaceted.

One mission of teaching is to render the complex and difficult understandable and manageable. This book attempts to provide a conceptual map of the territory of teaching reading that presents its most essential concepts in a clear, organized, and graphic way. The overall purpose is to explain the essentials of this subject in systematic terms, and to provide a visual framework that will be helpful in mentally organizing what can otherwise be a buzz of concepts, terminology, and unresolved issues. Therefore, this book should be of assistance both to those relatively new to the subject and to those whose more advanced knowledge of the subject is unsystematic.

In order to accomplish this purpose, the contents of this book are necessarily selective. We focus here on a basic understanding of key concepts to which many other concepts and issues in the field are related. This is not to subjugate the importance of those other concepts and issues, but to emphasize their antecedents. No one book could hope to do equal justice to all the facets of this field, and this book attempts to do justice to only a select few that form the foundation of knowledge in the field.

A related feature of this book is its "big picture," wide-perspective view. The focus on essential concepts invites broad application. The concepts presented here can be applied to teaching reading in a wide variety of ways at a wide variety of grade levels and to situations outside of schools, although most of the discussion is necessarily related to elementary reading. Large-scale research reports, reviews, and syntheses of research are cited more than individual studies that may be limited in generalizability. Of particular importance is the historical perspective taken here.

This perspective is that the essentials of teaching reading cannot be truly grasped without a knowledge of their historical development and attempts to systematically organize them. Our emphasis on history is not for purposes of background alone, but to make the reader appreciative of two important points:

- All current practices are modified versions of earlier practices, and practices that will emerge in the future will in all probability have predecessors. This understanding alone will help the reader to avoid one of the problems that has perennially beset the field: the belief that the discovery of the "one best method" for teaching reading is just over the next hill, and the faddish pursuit of this hope.
- Efforts to systematize the knowledge in this field have been few and have met with limited success so far.

We begin our wide-perspective treatment with a brief review of previous efforts to systematize the knowledge base of teaching reading. Unfamiliar terms are briefly defined in this chapter and more extensively developed throughout the book.

EFFORTS TO SYSTEMATIZE KNOWLEDGE OF TEACHING READING

Bringing order to the knowledge in any field is a critical scholarly activity. A classification system, or taxonomy, is central to every branch of science including the social sciences. Understanding the physical world began with schemes as simple as the ancient Greek division of the four elemental substances—earth, air, fire, and water—and grew into the periodic table of the elements. The classification system for animals and plants originated by Aristotle contained but a few categories that eventually evolved into today's comprehensive biological taxonomy of kingdom, phylum, class, order, family, genus, and species. Taxonomies of educational objectives have been developed (see Chapter 3). These classification systems are far more than an academic exercise. Such systems afford the advantage of precise communication among scholars and serve as a basis for further development in the field, including their own revision or replacement. Perhaps of no less importance is the conceptual framework they provide for those learning the field.

Efforts to produce classification systems and conceptual frameworks for the methods and approaches to teaching reading are actually fairly recent. After reviewing the whole history of the teaching of reading up to his own time, Huey (1908, p. 265) was able to provide only a short summary of the methods then in use: "The methods of learning to read that are in common use to-day may be classed as alphabetic, phonic, phonetic, word, sentence, and combination methods" (see below). In 1949, the International Bureau of Education of the United Nations Economic and Social Council (UNESCO) reported the results of a 45-nation survey that classified the teaching of reading into three categories (International Bureau of Education, 1949, pp. 24–25):

1. *Synthetic methods.* These include the alphabetical method, all the various phonic and phonetic methods, and the methods of direct reading of syllables.
2. *Analytic methods.* Among the variations of these methods, also called ideo-visual and sentence (or "global") may be included those which begin with the word, sentence, or story.
3. *Analytic–synthetic methods.* These methods are based on the word or sentence, and the most characteristic of them is the so-called common words method.

4

These methods were essentially the same as Huey's. With synthetic methods children first learn about letters (the alphabet) and speech sounds (phonetics) and put these together (phonics) to build syllables, words, and sentences. With analytic methods, children begin by seeing meaningful wholes (ideo-visual units) such as words, sentences, and stories connected with their everyday lives (common words). They then analyze these into successively smaller language units such as syllables, letters, and sounds. Analytic–synthetic methods combined these two approaches in some way.

Gray (1956) reported the results of another UNESCO study of the international status of teaching reading. He saw difficulty with the earlier three-method classification because he found disagreement regarding the class to which particular methods belonged. Alternatively, Gray described a historical dialectic wherein the analytic and synthetic methods were the earlier opposing approaches, and the newer combination (or eclectic) approach was a synthesis of the two that was enjoying increasing international acceptance.

In 1973, Downing published a study of comparative reading in 13 different countries including Argentina, Denmark, Finland, France, Germany, Great Britain, Hong Kong, India, Israel, Japan, Sweden, the United States, and the Soviet Union. These countries were selected as having noteworthy differences in language, orthography, culture, and educational systems. Downing determined that events since 1956 had not borne out Gray's contention of a growing acceptance of eclecticism. In fact, Downing determined that no method or synthesis of methods was clearly in favor anywhere in the world. The same debates about teaching reading were found in all countries, regardless of writing system, cultural characteristics, or educational traditions. Despite these differences, Downing (1973, p. 149) identified a universal continuum of methods of teaching reading:

Atomistic decoding and meaningful chunking represent its two extremes. Whether one is dealing with letters that represent phonemes, or a syllabary that signals the relevant sound group, or logographs that signify morphemic units, the same alternatives are available. One can begin by emphasizing the atoms of language, for instance, either in the separate letters of written words in English or in the radicals of Chinese logographs. Or one can put the emphasis on the larger chunks of written language that convey linguistic meaning. In parallel with this, the alternative emphases are the *mechanics* of the decoding task versus its *communicative function.*

Downing was describing the distinction between an emphasis on decoding and an emphasis on meaning in teaching reading, not dissimilar to Gray's earlier distinction between synthetic and analytic methods. Downing (1973, p. 158) also suggested three universal dimensions of general education that affected the teaching of reading. These dimensions were (1) child-centered versus curriculum-centered thinking, (2) formal versus informal approaches, and (3) individualized versus mass teaching techniques. However, Downing found that aligning these general education dimensions with the dimension of teaching reading was difficult because, like Gray, he encountered different definitions of the terms by different users.

That problem has continued to challenge those who have tried to bring order to the field. Chall (1967) classified beginning reading methods into two broad categories she called *code emphasis* and *meaning emphasis*. This distinction was generally similar to Gray's and Downing's. Chall also found that methods were classified into different categories by different authorities, and that teachers and researchers frequently seemed to violate their own theoretical assumptions in practice.

In his comprehensive review of the literature on reading sponsored by the United States Office of Education, Corder (1971, p. 63) expanded on Chall's categories and classified methods as:

1. Meaning emphasis
2. Code emphasis
   a. synthetic
   b. analytic

3. Linguistic
4. Modified alphabet
5. Responsive environment
6. Programmed learning
7. Individualized reading
8. Language experience
9. Eclectic or author's own

Definitions and discussions of these methods are supplied later in this book (Chapter 2, Chapter 6), but for now the alert reader will see similarities between this list and Downing's various dimensions. Corder (1971, p. 68) further identified five major psychological concepts that were pertinent to the body of knowledge unique to the profession of education:

1. Individual differences
2. Maturation and physical growth and development
3. Motivational structure
4. Learning theory
5. Socialization theory

However useful all these categories were for reviewing the literature on teaching reading, ultimately they were lists of topics rather than taxonomies of clearly distinguishable classes. The overlap among many terms in each list was substantial. Furthermore, the many possible combinations of methods and psychological emphases (over 45) precluded any reduction to a scheme of relationships among a few key concepts. Corder (1971, p. 128) concluded that ultimately all methods may reduce to "eclectic or author's own," the last category on his list of methods:

Thus under this latter conception, as many methods of reading instruction may exist as are created by the interactions of particular children with a particular teacher. The teacher, in essence, must invent a reading method for every child in her class every year.

Like Gray and Downing, both Chall and Corder encountered the challenging problem of finding a consistent framework for describing methods and approaches. Specificity was lacking. Terminology was often vague, inconsistent, and overlapping. Methods ranged from names of specific sets of materials to classroom organization practices to whole philosophies. We will return to the work of Gray, Downing, Chall, and Corder in later chapters.

Other efforts yielded incremental progress toward solving this problem. Goodman and Page (1978, p. 10) attempted to "bring some order to the chaos Corder found" by developing a set of 89 characteristics of reading programs such as the language unit emphasized (letter or sound, word, phrase, sentence, story), level of comprehension emphasized (literal or beyond), role of the teacher, role of the student, theory of learning employed, theory of language employed, and so on. These variables were combined in different theoretical ways in a comparison of several middle-grade reading programs of the day.

The most productive combination was to group the characteristics into nine theoretical categories. Three of the nine categories involved the missions of teaching reading: (1) producing the spoken analog of the printed language, (2) reconstructing the author's message, (3) constructing knowledge about the author's message. Another three categories involved views of language and learning: (1) innate, (2) behavioristic, (3) cognitive. Another three categories involved the locus of control and purpose for reading: (1) the text, (2) the teacher, (3) the reader. This conceptual framework resulted in a $3 \times 3 \times 3$ matrix of 27 different possible combinations (e.g., teacher-controlled, behavioristic, production of the spoken analog; innate, reader-controlled, construction of knowledge; etc.). Because each of the nine categories was further comprised of a subset of the 89 original characteristics, this framework was ponderous to understand and apply. It was, however, used with high reliability by specially trained raters in comparing several widely used commercial reading programs.

A refinement of this system attempted by this author (Sadoski, 1982) reduced the number of characteristics to a more manageable

8

number. We will explain and update that system throughout this book, so it will not be detailed here. It has been applied with moderate reliability by undergraduate students and classroom teachers to widely used commercial reading programs with efficiency.

Another attempt to bring order to models of teaching reading was attempted by Stahl and Hayes (1997). They examined 13 models of teaching reading that had emerged over the previous 20 years (e.g., direct instruction, whole language, cognitive strategy instruction, sociocultural models, reader response, Success for All, Reading Recovery). These conceptual models ranged along a continuum from highly structured, task-analytic models to child-centered, holistic models. Each model was compared on five points: (1) a description of the model, (2) how that model defined reading and teaching, (3) a description of a typical classroom, (4) its research base, and (5) needed future research.

In summarizing this attempt at categorization, Stahl and Hayes (1997) concluded that the models were complex and defied simple categorization. In fact, they found that there was much blending between models, especially where practice was concerned. Furthermore, they acknowledged, like Corder, that ultimately teachers hold their own models of reading that are often more eclectic than academic models. The problem of defining a comprehensive and useful conceptual framework for teaching reading remains a complex and challenging one.

THE STRUCTURE OF THIS BOOK

This book is structured by four essential questions:

- Why do we teach reading?
- What do we teach when we teach reading?
- How do we teach reading?
- How well do we teach reading?

One or more chapters are devoted to answering each of these questions.

Chapter 2 provides historical background on major contemporary approaches and methods. Beginning with the way reading was taught and learned in ancient Greece and Rome, the chapter traces major changes and developments in teaching reading with an emphasis on 20th-century America. The reader will be introduced to the evolution of many essential concepts in the teaching of reading such as decoding to speech, comprehending meaning, and responding to the meanings evoked by the text. The reader will learn that the teaching of reading is not always dominated by the teacher, but can be dependent on programs of materials or on the efforts and motivations of readers themselves. The reader will learn that new methods, approaches, and programs often have historical ancestors.

Chapter 3 deals with an issue too often excluded from books on this subject: the goals of teaching reading. This chapter addresses the *why* of teaching reading. The treatment of goals draws on broad learning taxonomies and large-scale research on the reasons people read and need to read. The goals themselves cover both the cognitive and the affective domains of learning. The chapter ends with the argument that any complete curriculum in reading needs to address all these goals.

Chapters 4, 5, and 6 together present the conceptual map of teaching reading that is the heart of this book. This conceptual map, or framework, is both reductionist and expansionist. It attempts to reduce the essentials of teaching reading to a manageable number of concepts, describe them in detail, and coordinate those concepts into a graphic framework. Reductionism is useful for organizing knowledge about a subject, the stated purpose of this book. However, there is danger in reductionism, as previous efforts to systematize knowledge in this field show. The reader is invited to think expansively about the application of this framework to a variety of teaching situations. The reader is also invited to think expansively about the flaws in this framework, to find what doesn't neatly fit, to question its order. The fact that current methods have evolved from earlier ones should not imply that there are no new ideas under the sun.

Chapter 4 addresses the *what* of teaching reading. In this chapter, three fundamental competencies of reading are presented: decoding, comprehension, and response. Each is defined in detail, and then the three are cast as benchmarks on a continuum between input from the print and input from the reader. This continuum forms one of two main dimensions of the framework.

Chapter 5 addresses the *how* of teaching reading. This chapter presents a dichotomy between *instruction* and *education*. Using classical definitions of these terms, these two poles form the ends of another continuum that is the second dimension of the conceptual framework. Three general teaching approaches are identified that lean toward one pole or the other: program-controlled teaching/learning, teacher-controlled teaching/learning, and reader-controlled teaching/learning. These are cast as benchmarks on the second continuum.

Chapter 6 coordinates the dimensions introduced in Chapter 4 and Chapter 5 into the overall conceptual map. Different broad, opposing territories on the map are identified as representative of the *skills approach* and the *holistic approach*. These territories are characterized by assigning selected, well-known, well-researched methods and approaches to them. The historically recurring concept of a balanced approach is noted.

Chapter 7 further discusses the *how* of teaching reading through a balanced approach that is consistent with much contemporary research and thought on the subject. Like all balanced approaches, those suggested here are a combination of practices derived from the skills approach and the holistic approach. The few suggested combinations are not presented as a surefire recipe or foolproof formula, but as a rational set of exemplars guided by some commonsense and empirically defensible principles and practices. Perhaps the most appealing aspect of a balanced approach is the teacher creativity it invites.

Chapter 8 addresses the question *how well?* This chapter reviews large-scale summaries of the achievement of reading ability in the United States over more than a century, and the relative effectiveness of the skills and holistic approaches in producing that achievement. Given the passionate public debate on this subject, the reader may be surprised at the picture presented in this chapter. Like much else in this book, it will hopefully organize thought on the subject and provide a challenge for further thought.

REFERENCES

Chall, J. S. (1967). *Learning to read: The great debate*. New York: McGraw-Hill.

Corder, R. (1971). *The information base for reading: A critical review of the information base for current assumptions regarding the status of instruction and achievement in the United States*. Educational Testing Service, U.S. Office of Education Project 0-9031, Final Report. (ERIC Document Reproduction Service No. ED 054 922)

Downing, J. (1973). *Comparative reading: Cross-national studies of behavior and processes in reading and writing*. New York: Macmillan.

Goodman, K. S., & Page, W. D. (1978). *Reading comprehension programs: Theoretical bases of reading instruction in the middle grades*. National Institute of Education, U.S. Department of Health, Education, and Welfare, Revised Final Report. (ERIC Document Reproduction Service No. ED 165 092)

Gray, W. S. (1956). *The teaching of reading and writing*. Paris: United Nations Economic and Social Council.

Huey, E. B. (1908). *The psychology and pedagogy of reading*. New York: Macmillan. (Reprinted 1968, Cambridge, MA: MIT Press)

International Bureau of Education. (1949). *The teaching of reading*. Paris: United Nations Economic and Social Council.

Sadoski, M. (1982). *A study of the theoretical bases of reading instruction and a comparison of programs*. Texas A&M University Instructional Research Laboratory Technical Paper No. R83001. (ERIC Document Reproduction Service No. ED 236 543)

Stahl, S. A., & Hayes, D. A. (1997). *Instructional models in reading*. Mahwah, NJ: Erlbaum.

CHAPTER 2

A Brief History
of Teaching Reading

This chapter provides a brief overview of the history of teaching reading, with an emphasis on the 20th century in the United States. It will deal with some major movements as interpreted by historians in the field (Fries, 1962; Huey, 1908; Mathews, 1966; Smith, 2002). Emphasis is placed on some key concepts that are developed into a framework in the chapters that follow. It has been wisely said that those who do not know history are doomed to repeat it, and this surely seems true in the teaching of reading, for opposing points of view have swung in and out of favor like the proverbial pendulum.

Actually, the fervent debate over the teaching of reading that has marked recent history is relatively new. In fact, if the history of teaching reading in fully alphabetic languages was compressed into 1 year, the first significant changes in teaching methods would not come about until November and December, and the great majority of significant debate and change in methods would not come about until the last 3 weeks of December.

THE ALPHABET
AND THE ALPHABET METHOD

Alphabetic writing, where written symbols stand for speech sounds, first emerged in the Middle East more than 5,000 years ago. Our Roman alphabet today descends from the symbols used by the Phoenicians, a trading nation on the eastern Mediterranean, who needed a way of efficiently recording commercial transactions. The letters they used were a hybrid between pictograms (shapes representing objects) and letters representing speech sounds. The Greeks traded with the Phoenicians and adopted the Phoenician alphabet with some modifications roughly 3,000 years ago. The Greek alphabet was in turn adopted with modifications in Italy first by the Etruscans and later by the Romans. No significant reforms in the principles of alphabetic writing have taken place since then. Our contemporary English alphabet evolved from the Roman alphabet with only minor changes.

The earliest method for teaching reading in a fully alphabetic language also dates back to ancient Greece and Rome. That method is the *spelling method* or the *alphabet (ABC) method*. Greek and Roman teachers drilled their students in reciting the alphabet over and over, forward and backward. Students sang it in simple melodies and arranged tiles or blocks with the letters on them until they knew the alphabet well. (The alphabet song and alphabet blocks are still with us today.) After learning the alphabet, early students would be drilled in syllabaries composed of simple vowel–consonant combinations (*ab, eb, ib, ob, ub*) in which they would say the names of the letters and then pronounce the syllable. The students would eventually advance to lists of words that they spelled, pronounced, and memorized in preparation for reading particular texts. With few modifications, this method was employed until well into the 19th century in Europe and America. Until then, few other approaches were proposed, and no other approach was widely accepted. Virtually all changes in teaching reading have come about since then.

Reading during the era of the spelling method was heavily influenced by the idea that reading is the act of orally repeating an author's very words. The Greeks and Romans attached primacy to the spoken word and to the art of oratory. Writing was seen as a distinctly secondary system, useful mainly to record a speaker's words for those who were absent from the actual speech. The Greek philosopher Socrates, feeling that the discovery of the alphabet would destroy the use of memory in learning, used oral language exclusively and wrote nothing. Even private reading was usually done orally, or in a murmur. Saint Augustine, visiting with Bishop Ambrose of Milan in the year 384, commented on his peculiar habit of reading silently to himself. The pervasive emphasis on oral reading lasted well into the 19th century in America, where reading was defined in an 1829 reading textbook as "*Reading is talking from a book*" (Leavitt, cited in Smith, 2002). Reading lessons of that day typically began with articulation and enunciation exercises and stressed accurate oral reading exclusively.

Teaching by the alphabet method emphasized the sequence *letters to words and reading*, with decoding to speech as the primary goal. The alphabet method fell from use in America in the late 1800s, but decoding to speech and formal oral reading as the primary goals of teaching reading persisted years after the demise of the alphabet method.

EARLY INNOVATIONS IN EUROPE

Some of the first departures from the alphabet method came about during the early 1500s in Europe. In 1527, the German teacher Valentin Ickelsamer prepared an introductory reading book called *The Shortest Way to Reading* in which he expounded a new method. This method involved having students first learn to isolate speech sounds, then learn the letters that stood for them, referring to con-

15

ventional letter sounds as letter "names." Students began reading by "naming" the letters (pronouncing their sounds) quickly together. This may have been the beginning of the *synthetic phonics method,* one of the first significant departures from the alphabet method.

Ickelsamer's method was not widely accepted at the time, with one critic of the day referring to his school as a "babble factory" (Mathews, 1966). However, his work may have inspired other innovators. John Hart advanced a similar method of teaching reading in English in a 1570 publication with the happy title *A Methode or Comfortable Beginning for All Unlearned, Whereby They May Bee Taught to Read English, in a Very Short Time, with Pleasure.* Hart attacked the alphabet method and called for a phonic approach using the speech sounds of the letters rather than their names. Hart's method also used special diacritical marks for the letters so that each letter would represent only one sound and each sound one letter (Fries, 1962). This method was not widely accepted at the time either.

A different departure from the alphabet method came when visual alphabet books in the 1500s began to associate letters with pictures. These books could be seen as using pictures in the service of learning letters. However, in 1658, the Moravian educator Johan Amos Comenius published *The Orbis Sesnusalium Pictus: A World of Things Obvious to the Senses Drawn in Pictures* in Nuremberg, Germany. The origins and influence of this book are an interesting history in themselves (Sadoski & Paivio, 2001). It is considered to be the first fully illustrated reading book and the beginning of the *word method* in teaching reading (Huey, 1908). It also was one of the earliest methods to place the comprehension of meaning on the same level as decoding in beginning reading. Much of what came to be widely accepted centuries later in the teaching of reading can be traced back to the Comenius and *The Orbis.*

Each lesson in the book was an illustration of some familiar scene such as a farm, stable, or shop with various objects numbered. On the facing page, the text referred to the numbered objects with explanations in parallel columns of English and Latin (Figure 2.1). Comenius contended that by matching things with words

VI.

Aër

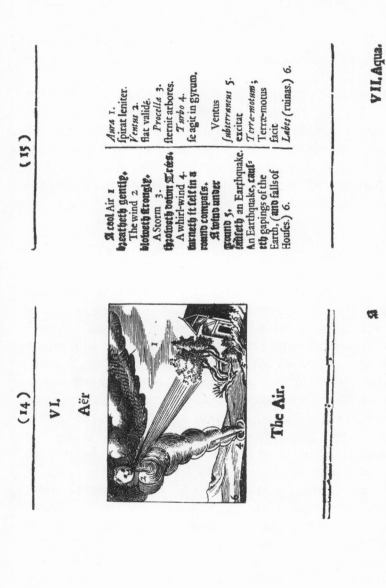

The Air.

A cool Air 1
breatheth gently.
The wind 2
bloweth strongly.
A Storm 3.
throweth down Trees.
A whirl-wind 4.
turneth it self in a
round compass.
A wind under
ground 5.
causeth an Earthquake.
An Earthquake, caus-
eth gapings of the
Earth, (and falls of
Houses.) 6.

Aura 1.
spirat leniter.
Ventus 2.
flat validè.
Procella 3.
sternit arbores.
Turbo 4.
se agit in gyrum.

*Ventus
subterraneus* 5.
excitat
Terræ-motum;
Terræ-motus
facit
Labes (ruinas.) 6.

VII. Aqua.

FIGURE 2.1. Adjacent pages from a 1659 English version of *The Orbis Sensualium Pictus*. Note the catchwords at the bottom of each page. Some old books printed a word at the bottom of each page that began the next page both as a guide for assembling the pages in binding and to hold the reader's attention. *Aqua* is Latin for water, the subject of the next lesson.

17

learning to read could be accomplished without the rote drill of the spelling method. However, *The Orbis* also included a picture alphabet that taught phonic associations, such as a picture of a growling dog for the letter *r*. The use of meaningful words and individual letter sounds together may also have been the precursor of *analytic phonics* (breaking down known words into their individual sound–letter units).

This method shifted the emphasis in teaching from *letters to words and reading* to *words to letters and reading*, with both decoding and comprehension as goals. While *The Orbis* method did not replace the alphabet method, it enjoyed great popularity in Europe for more than 100 years. Using familiar words as the basis for beginning reading instruction became known as the "normal words" or "common words" method of teaching reading.

THE SCENE IN EARLY AMERICA

Teaching reading in colonial America was done by the alphabet method with a distinctly religious mission. Our earliest reading books were called "primers" (pronounced with the medieval short *i*). These books were not named for being the books from which reading was first learned, but from the religious content of the earliest primers, which included the primary scriptural essentials considered necessary for salvation. The spelling method was employed in the colonial primers, complete with the letters of the alphabet, a syllabary ranging from two letters to multisyllable words, and then sentences and verses. After learning to read with the primer, the student would advance directly to the Bible.

The most popular primer was the *New England Primer*, published in Boston in 1690 (Figure 2.2). It dominated the teaching of reading for a century. Along with the Bible, it was one of the most common books in colonial America (Huey, 1908). Its grim content can be described as morality and mortality. The horrors of death, damnation, and decay were dwelt upon. The child's prayer

Easy Syllables for Children.

Ab	eb	ib	ob	ub
ac	ec	ic	oc	uc
ad	ed	id	od	ud
af	ef	if	of	uf
am	em	im	om	um
au	en	in	on	un
ap	ep	ip	op	up
ar	er	ir	or	ur
as	es	is	os	us
at	et	it	ot	ut
ba	be	bi	bo	bu
ca	ce	ci	co	cu
da	de	di	do	du
ha	he	hi	ho	hu
pa	pe	pi	po	pu
sa	se	si	so	su
ta	te	ti	to	tu
bla	ble	bli	blo	blu
cla	cle	cli	clo	clu

Words of One Syllable.

Act	eat	kite	said
add	egg	knife	schoo
air	fall	lad	seat
all	for	lamb	that
and	fork	land	them
bad	free	man	this
ball	gate	may	urn
bench	give	more	use
bird	gold	nail	vain
cake	hall	name	vast
came	hat	old	walk
card	his	one	well
cup	ice	out	went
dark	join	pen	when
dead	joy	play	which
deaf	judge	poor	year
dirt	just	queen	your
each	keep	rain	youth
earth	king	read	zeal

FIGURE 2.2. Adjacent pages from the *New England Primer*, an 1826 edition that is identical to editions published back to the 1600s. After first learning the alphabet, students drilled on spelling and pronouncing syllables and one-syllable words.

"Now I lay me down to sleep" was included in this primer and is somewhat representative of its religious content. A religious catechism was also included. Reading lessons were typically performed orally, with accuracy, and often in unison in keeping with religious observance. The rote memorization of verses and passages was stressed.

Spelling books competed with primers and eventually replaced them in the 1700s. Noah Webster (of dictionary fame) published the *American Spelling Book* in 1783, and it became the most widely used textbook of its day (Figure 2.3). Its sales throughout history may have reached 100 million copies (Mathews, 1966). It was actually the first of a series of three books designed to introduce spelling and reading, teach grammar, and provide lessons for advanced reading and elocution. Although the second and third books did not enjoy the popularity of the first, the series constituted the first set of consecutive readers in America, a development that would flourish.

The "old blue-back speller" employed the alphabet method but also incorporated some synthetic phonics (associating sounds with letters and blending the sounds into words). The book began with extensive directions on pronunciation for teachers and schoolmasters to model for the children, "for if all instructors pronounced words with correctness and uniformity, there would be little danger that their pupils would acquire vicious habits of pronunciation." This book is often credited with producing a common U.S. dialect distinct from the English spoken in Britain. The book included the alphabet, a syllabary, long lists of words broken into their syllables, verses, and fables. Shorter, more common words were presented first, and longer and irregular words were presented later. The verses and fables were moralistic, religious, and patriotic in keeping with the new nationalism after the American Revolution. In reading lessons, rote memorization was replaced with eloquent oral reading that might inspire readers and listeners to respond with patriotic fervor (Smith, 2002).

32	*An Easy Standard of Pronunciation.*
sa cer do tal	mem o ran dum
su per vi sor	o ri ent al
ac ci dent al	or na ment al
ar o mat ic	pan e gyr ic
cal i man co	pred e ces sor
det ri ment al	sci en tif ic
en er get ic	sys tem at ic
fun da ment al	cor res pŏnd ent
in nu en do	hor i zon tal
mal e fac tor	u ni vẽr sal
man i fes to	un der stand ing
at mos pher ic	o ver whelm ing

⁎ Having proceeded through tables, composed of easy words from one to four syllables, let the learner begin the following tables, which consist of more difficult words. In these the child will be much assisted by a knowledge of the figures and the use of the Italics.

If the instructor should think it useful to let his pupils read some of the easy lessons, before they have finished spelling, he may divide their studies—let them spell one part of the day, and read the other.

TABLE XII.

Difficult and irregular Monosyllables.

I would recommend this table to be read sometimes across the page.

Bay	clay	rail	flail	brain
day	way	frail	snail	chain
hay	ray	wail	laird	grain
lay	bray	mail	aid	slain
say	stray	nail	maid	train
may	slay	trail	stair	rain
pay	spay	bail	swear	main
pray	jail	ail	wear	plain
sway	pail	hail	bear	sprain
fray	sail	tail	tear	stain

		An Easy Standard of Pronunciation.			33
twain	tray	change	squeal	creed	
vain	gay	strange	beer	heed	
wain	slay	blaze	peer	mead	
paint	play	be	deer	knead	
quaint	beard	pea	fear	reed	
plaint	date	sea	dear	bleed	
aim	tale	tea	bear	breed	
claim	staid	flea	near	plead	
main	laid	yea	rear	deem	
waif	paid	key	veer	seem	
stage	braid	leap	drear	cream	
gauge	air	neap	clear	dream	
plague	chair	reap	shear	stream	
vague	fair	cheap	steer	beam	
bait	hair	heap	bier	steam	
great	pair	steel	tier	seam	
gait	lain	kneel	year	gleam	
wait	pain	teal	cheer	scream	
plait	strain	feel	heard	fleam	
strait	gain	keel	blear	fream	
graze	blain	deal	ear	ream	
praise	drain	heal	sear	team	
raise	fain	meal	smear	least	
baise	faint	peel	spear	feast	
raze	taint	reel	tear	yeast	
maize	saint	seal	queer	beast	
shave	trait	steal	deed	priest	
brave	haste	veal	feed	east	
knave	paste	weal	need	reef	
break	waste	zeal	weed	grief	
steak	baste	peal	bead	brief	
spray	chaste	beal	lead	chief	
stay	taste	ceil	read	deaf	
gray	traipse	eel	seed	leaf	

FIGURE 2.3. Adjacent pages from an 1894 edition of the *American Spelling Book*. After drilling on spelling and pronouncing phonetically regular words of from one through four syllables, students drilled on spelling and reading phonetically irregular words. The directions to the teacher indicate that spelling was supposed to precede reading up to this point.

CHANGES AND REFORMS IN THE 1800s

The 1800s brought many changes to the U.S. scene. The influential educational reformer Horace Mann visited European schools in 1843 and returned to launch a scathing attack on the alphabet method. He had observed the normal words and synthetic phonics methods in Prussian schools and believed that the use of the alphabet method and spelling books in teaching reading was vexing, harmful, and inferior. A debate ensued between Mann and his critics regarding the place of letters and their names, phonic values, and words in the teaching of reading. The alphabet method continued to be widely used, but the word method and the phonic method grew in popularity in the United States during the 1800s, with several popular beginning reading series devoted to them. These readers also showed increased concern for the attitudes and interests of children.

The most popular readers of this period were the McGuffey readers. William H. McGuffey was a midwestern professor credited with being the first author to produce a carefully graded series consisting of one reader for each elementary grade (Smith, 2002). First appearing in 1836, the McGuffey readers were immediately popular. Probably 80% of the students of the time used them, and as many as 120 million sets were sold. Early editions stressed the phonic method. Later, revised editions also promoted the new methods emerging in the United States. By 1879, the McGuffey readers provided teachers with a format for teaching by the phonic method, the word method, or both (p. ii):

> This **First Reader** may be used in teaching reading by any of the methods in common use; but it is especially adapted to the Phonic method, and Word Method, or a combination of the two.
>
> I. **Phonic Method**.—First teach the elementary sounds and their representatives, the letters marked with diacriticals, as they occur in the lessons; then, the formation of words by the combination of these sounds. . . . Having read a few lessons in this manner, be-

gin to teach the names of the letters and the spelling of words, and require the groups "a man," "the man," "a pen," "the pen," to be read as a good reader would pronounce single words.

II. When one of the letters in the combinations *ou* or *ow*, is marked in the words at the head of the reading exercises, the other is silent. If neither is marked, the two letters present a dipthong. All other unmarked vowels in the vocabularies, when *in combination*, are silent letters. In slate or blackboard work, the silent letters may be canceled.

III. **Word Method.**—Teach pupils to identify at sight the words placed at the head of the reading exercises, and to read these exercises without hesitation. Having read a few lessons, begin to teach the names of the letters and the spelling of the words.

IV. **Word Method and Phonic Method Combined.**—Teach the pupil to identify words and read sentences, as above. Having read a few lessons in this manner, begin to use the Phonic Method, combining it with the Word Method, by first teaching the words in each lesson *as words*; then, the elementary sounds, the names of the letters, and the spelling.

These teaching directions indicated the movement away from the alphabet method, although some of it remained. They summarize much of the change in the history of teaching reading until that time. Early lessons in McGuffey's primer (Figure 2.4) emphasized the alphabet, letter pronunciations, and the repetition of words of two or three letters in brief texts. Diacritical marks were used with letters to aid pronunciation, as they had been by John Hart some 300 years before. Subsequent lessons gradually introduced longer words and texts.

An increasing emphasis was placed on meaning and comprehension beyond the primers. Early editions of the McGuffey readers contained simple comprehension questions after the passage, often designed to teach some moral point (e.g., Does not God always watch over the good?). This was in keeping with the moralistic and didactic emphasis seen in reading and spelling books from the earliest times in America. Passages from or about the Bible were

LESSON III.

ĭt   hĭṣ   pĕn   hănd
a   ĭn   hăṣ   măn

           p   h   ě

The   man.   A   pen.

The man has a pen.
Is the pen in his hand?
It is in his hand.

FIGURE 2.4. Lesson 3 from *McGuffey's First Eclectic Reader* (rev. ed., 1879). By this lesson, beginners were expected to spell out, sound out, and read phrases and sentences as well as individual words using the eclectic method.

used, but so were passages from British and American literature. The upper-grade readers especially had a high literary standard, containing long and difficult passages from classic authors such as Homer, Shakespeare, and Longfellow. To many Americans on the rural frontier, this was all the literature they ever saw.

Another new method to emerge in the late 1800s was the *sentence method*. A major proponent was George L. Farnham, who published his pamphlet *The Sentence Method* in 1881. This manual became widely used in the teacher training institutions of the day. This method proposed the sentence as the base unit of expression. Sentences were taught as wholes and later analyzed into words and letters. Farnham maintained that the first aim of reading was "thought" reading, by which he meant silently comprehending the thoughts expressed in print with the least possible consciousness of the words used. He felt that undue emphasis on spelling, phonics, and eloquent oral reading resulted in thinking pronunciations while reading silently, a habit he held to be laborious and destructive of reading extended texts (Fries, 1962). This approach emphasized comprehension from the start and might be seen as a *reading to words and letters* approach.

However, elaborate phonic methods were also developed during this time, partly in reaction to reports that the word and sentence methods failed to produce independent readers. One such method was the *synthetic method* described by Rebecca Pollard in 1889. She stressed that the sounds of the letters should be taught first with no guesswork, reference to pictures, or waiting for a story line to develop the thought. She maintained that the word method and the sentence method were incompatible. The main goal of beginning readers was to be able to pronounce words for themselves in new reading material. Pollard used innovative techniques to appeal to the interests of children through songs and mental images (Smith, 2002). The sound of *r* was associated with a growling dog, the sound of *ch* with the sound of a steam train chugging, and so on (a practice that can be traced back to *The Orbis*). However, an eminent reading scholar of the day, Edmund Burke Huey (1908, p.

284) referred to this method as "a crime against childhood that cannot long be suffered." Debates about reading methods were becoming acerbic.

Huey disparaged early use of alphabet and phonic methods and advocated the sentence method, reporting that it produced excellent results at first. However, he also found that it often broke down when students attempted to read unfamiliar text independently. In practice, teachers of the day who used this method often supplemented it with some amount of phonics. Eclectic or balanced approaches to teaching reading were becoming known, and published reading series of the day often combined word, phonic, and sentence methods to give teachers many options.

Another method praised by Huey was a precursor of the language experience approach (see Chapters 5 and 6) taught in the schools of Francis Parker, a colleague of the philosopher and progressive educator John Dewey. Called the *activity approach*, it taught children how to read as they had learned to talk. This method involved writing the names of objects that were of interest to the children as these words were spoken. Both individual words and sentences were used. The words and sentences grew out of the children's own investigations. The words and sentences were erased shortly afterward and the children were prompted to reproduce them with the request, "Say it with the chalk." Oral reading began with children reading the sentences they had written. Phonic analysis was taught through the slow pronunciation of easy words after children had developed a sight vocabulary and the ability to read fairly long sentences.

Parker attributed this approach to *The Orbis* and sought to instill literacy as a natural adjunct to the exploration of content, not as a subject itself. Parker (1894/1969, p. 221) also stressed comprehension and response from the beginning, stating that *"reading is thinking, not the pronunciation of words."* But Parker was hardly without his detractors; critics labeled his schools "fad factories," and decried the activity approach as "glorified mudpie making" (Mathews, 1966).

The growth of interest in meaning and comprehension coincided with a general movement in U.S. society at this time. This movement was the popularization of intellectual culture that took the form of interest in literature. Educators became keenly interested in the *what* of reading as well as the *how*. Curriculum materials as early as 1880 showed an increasing concern for developing interest, appreciation, and taste in reading through exposure to quality literature.

In 1890, Charles W. Eliot, then president of Harvard University, attacked the school readers of the day on these grounds. He revealed a personal study showing that a high school graduate reading at a moderate rate could read in 46 hours all of what elementary school students were called upon to read in 6 years. He pointed out that most of this material was written for school books and lacked any worthwhile content. He called for the use of true literature in its place. The use of children's literature in teaching reading has again become quite popular today (e.g., Norton, 2003).

The new emphasis on literature combined with the principles of the sentence method to produce the *story method* in teaching reading. Short works of literature suitable for children, such as folktales and fairy tales, were read to and with children until they became familiar with them. Children would memorize, dramatize, and finally read the stories. The texts would then be analyzed into thought groups, sentences, phrases, and words. Phonics was employed sparingly after stories were read. The use of familiar, repetitive stories such as "The Little Red Hen" and "The Three Billy Goats Gruff" proved well adapted to the interests and abilities of young children. Reading books using this method were often superbly illustrated.

Another aspect of the story method was the use of rhymes and poems that children learned by heart and later used as a self-reference for "looking up" words that they might have forgotten. The story method is a precursor of the patterned language or predictable books of today (see Chapter 6). Expressive oral reading for interpretation and literary response was stressed in reading lessons of the day.

By the end of the 19th century, popular approaches alternately emphasized *letters to words and reading,* or *words to letters and reading,* or *reading to words and letters* (cf. Mathews, 1966). The fundamental reading competencies of decoding, comprehension, and response had all gained established places in the teaching of reading. Teaching approaches centered on structured text materials, the teacher's judgment and choices, or the child's developing interests and abilities had all gained established places as well. The alphabet or spelling method was rapidly fading into history, having evolved into the phonic method. The comprehension of meaning and the appreciation of religious and literary text had always been an end goal of reading, but a new emphasis on meaning was being advocated from the earliest ages by some prominent scholars. The pendulum of decoding versus meaning had started swinging, with proponents of one method or the other assailing their opponents. The 20th century would bring still more changes.

THE EARLY 20TH CENTURY

The turn of the century marked a distinctive point in the teaching of reading. Reading was starting to be thought of as thinking. Prior to this time, memorization and oral expression were the first goals in teaching reading. Rather than being defined as "talking from a book," reading was now being defined differently: "The grasp of thought through the written characters is reading" (Laing, 1903, p. 65). Attention to comprehension and response as found in the sentence, story, and activity methods was gaining ground, although elaborate phonic methods found new popularity in reaction. Opposing sides in a debate had emerged, but oral reading was still the primary classroom method for both sides.

The period beginning about 1915 introduced new developments prompted by the first standardized tests in reading. The period was marked by scientific investigation into reading because measurement of the effectiveness of methods, materials, and practices could now be done with a degree of scientific objectivity. Among the strongest and earliest findings of these investigations was that silent reading was superior to oral reading in both speed and comprehension. This new view of reading called for a new pedagogy. Almost immediately, a sweeping reform replaced oral reading methods with silent reading methods, perhaps the most drastic change in method that had ever taken place (Smith, 2002).

Curriculum documents, professional books, teachers' manuals, and basal readers all reflected this shifted emphasis. The content of the readers changed accordingly. Reading literary selections for appreciation was not consistent with testing for comprehension and speed, so readers began to devote more pages to factual material. Consequently, reading more efficiently in a variety of content areas became increasingly valued. The use of tests also revealed that wide differences in reading ability existed in any grade, and concern for individual differences began to emerge. Testing also revealed that many children were having difficulty with reading, and the specialized branch of teaching reading known as remedial reading began. Still other research studies indicated that large differences existed in both adults and children in their attitudes, interests, and purposes in reading.

By 1925, the scene had changed broadly. A variety of goals in teaching reading were now valued including the development of attitudes, interests, and tastes; participation in recreation and public affairs in an increasingly literate society; and the stimulation of efficient thinking, informative learning, and appreciation through text. Methods emphasized silent reading for meaning and deemphasized teaching the mechanics of reading. However, two of the schools of thought that emerged in the 1800s had differing views about how meaningful reading should be taught and learned. One school grew from the *words to letters and reading* view, and the other grew from the *reading to words and letters* view.

The first school held that children should be given practice in a sequence of skills carefully planned by adults and set out in a graded series of readers ("basal" readers, the base or foundation of teaching reading). These programs began with familiar words in short, meaningful stories and proceeded to analytic phonics and other forms of word analysis and simultaneously to the comprehension of longer, more challenging passages. William S. Gray and Arthur I. Gates were prominent proponents of this position.

The second school of thought was the activity movement advanced by Francis Parker, John Dewey, and other progressive educators. This program held that learning to read best took place in an atmosphere of purposeful, child-centered exploration and activity. The activity approach grew in popularity in the early 20th century, but the number of schools that operated on anything like a pure version of the activity approach was always very small. In practice, the use of dictated language experience stories became a supplement to basal readers, and many basal reader teachers' manuals of this period recommended the practice.

A concern of those favoring a skills approach was exactly what skills should be taught and in what order. Although some broad distinctions were evident (e.g., word recognition, oral interpretation, comprehension, appreciation), a full classification had not yet been defined. A comprehensive theory of reading skills and their teaching was absent. One of the most influential efforts to classify and sequence reading skills was accomplished by William S. Gray at the University of Chicago.

One of the foremost authorities of his day, Gray had compiled professional curriculum documents from around the country in an effort to comprehensively describe the state of the teaching of reading. He headed the National Commission on Reading that in 1925 published an influential report proposing a program of reading with the broad goals noted earlier. Nearly every basal reading series and professional textbook soon adopted this view of reading. The report also noted that a complete classification of reading skills, habits, and attitudes had not been made, although a list of commonly taught skills was presented.

Starting in the 1930s and ending in the 1960s, Gray developed a comprehensive skills model of reading with four levels:

- Word perception, including pronunciation and meaning
- Comprehension, which included a "clear grasp of what is read"
- Reaction to and evaluation of ideas the author presents
- Assimilation of what is read, the fusion of existing knowledge and new information

Each level of the model was further subdivided, a subject detailed in Chapter 4. The influence of this model may be difficult to overstate because it became the theoretical foundation of the basal readers of the 1940s and 1950s, the school years of most of the huge "baby boom" generation that emerged after World War II. Due to its influence, we will describe the typical basal approach of the 1940s and 1950s in detail.

THE "CONVENTIONAL WISDOM"
OF THE MID-20TH CENTURY

The basal series of this era evolved from a series of books like the McGuffey readers, to be mastered as ability and education allowed, to a series of books carefully sequenced by grade. The starting place for reading was reading readiness in kindergarten or grade 1, in which students did workbook exercises in the visual discrimination of shapes including letter shapes, auditory discrimination of likenesses and differences in spoken words, letter tracing and learning the alphabet, interpreting wordless picture stories, and so on. The purpose was to ensure that children were well prepared for reading.

The next step, according to Gray's model, was word perception. This involved learning a sight vocabulary. The words included had been derived from frequency analyses of commonly read materials including reading books. The first-grade child proceeded lesson by lesson through two or three preprimers in which a set of words was systematically introduced and repeated in simple, illustrated stories. The progression continued through the primer and first reader in grade one, two readers in grade two, two readers in grade three, and one book per grade thereafter.

The *New Basic Readers* basal reader series authored by Gray and others in the 1940s and 1950s serves as a historic example. This was the series that introduced Dick, Jane, Sally, and their pets to the baby boom generation (Figure 2.5). The scrupulousness of the system for introducing and reinforcing words can be seen in the directions to the teacher in the first preprimer, *We Look and See* (Gray, Artley, & Arbuthnot, 1951, p. 48):

> Usefulness has determined the choice of the 17 words presented in *We Look and See*. A gradual introduction of these words plus unusual care in maintenance gives maximum opportunity for early reading success. There is no more than one new word per page, and there are no more than three new words in any story. Easy mastery is facilitated by bunched repetitions; no gap of more than five pages occurs between any two of the first five uses of a new word. At least seven more uses occur at spaced intervals throughout the book. Thus, in all, each word is used at least twelve times in *We Look and See*.

The books beyond continued this controlled introduction and repetition of sight vocabulary so that the three preprimers included a total of 58 words and the primer introduced 100 more. Learning to read was built on this base of sight vocabulary.

This approach was the *words to letters and reading* approach with some deemphasis on, but not elimination of, phonics and letter-level learning. It was essentially the normal words or word method, traceable back to *The Orbis*, enhanced by stimulus–response psychology. Because of the heavy emphasis on sight vocabulary, this came to be known as the "look–say" approach. This approach called for much oral recitation.

Comprehension was included from the start. Suggestions to the teacher in the three preprimers included many comprehension questions and comprehension activities including predicting story content from pictures and titles; following a sequence of events; in-

Oh, Jane.

See Spot and Tim.

See Spot run.

See funny Spot.

See funny Tim.

FIGURE 2.5. Page 34 from *We Look and See*, the first preprimer of the Scott-Foresman New Basic Reader Curriculum Foundation Series, 1951. This is the page where the baby-boom generation first encountered the immortal line "See Spot run." Note the systematic sight word repetition.

terpreting main ideas and supporting details; anticipating outcomes; recognizing the emotional reactions of characters; forming visual, auditory, and tactile images; and so on. Word recognition skills including analytic phonics were included in teacher's directions and students' workbooks.

Successive books in this series followed the controlled introduction of vocabulary such that the sixth-grade basal reader introduced 1,540 new words, but without the controlled repetition of the beginning books. Many of the sixth-grade words were challenging, unusual words (e.g., *chortled, bumptious, spatterdash*) in passages from children's classics such as *Robin Hood, Ben and Me*, and *The King of the Golden River*. Both fiction and nonfiction stories were included. Comprehension and response were developed in parallel with word perception abilities.

Oral reading and interpretation were included, with many lessons calling for orally interpreting lines with expression. However, silent reading always preceded oral reading, with the teacher guiding the children through the story page by page, asking questions, eliciting predictions, and encouraging children to project themselves into the story. Oral rereading was intended to reflect the understanding that the child derived when reading silently, and to unify plot, action, and conversation. Suggested supplementary activities typically included dramatization, artistic renderings, reading related stories and poems, analyzing rhyming words for phonic similarities, playing word games, flash card drills on words and phrases, and workbook activities that reinforced both comprehension and word recognition.

During the middle of the 20th century as many as 90% of all schoolchildren were learning to read from one or another basal reader series, all of which were similar to Gray's. Chall (1967) referred to this approach as the "conventional wisdom" of the period from the 1930s through the 1950s. Although the basals later changed in important ways (e.g., they included more ethnic and racial diversity, more use of children's literature, more supplementary writing, less vocabulary control), the model developed by Gray remained their foundation for decades and is still evident in basals today.

ALTERNATIVES TO THE
CONVENTIONAL WISDOM

The conventional wisdom of the look–say basals was not without critics. In 1955, Rudolf Flesch, a professor of rhetoric, published *Why Johnny Can't Read and What You Can Do about It*. This surprise best-seller condemned the look–say approach and advocated a return to phonics first. Flesch's reason for his fervent advocacy of phonics was essentially the same as Rebecca Pollard's was in 1889: a dissatisfaction with promoting "guesswork" as opposed to the specific identification and recognition of letters, sounds, and words. Flesch was not a reading scholar, but his rhetoric struck a chord with the U.S. public, and a concern for phonics resurged. This resurgence took the form of increased attention to phonics in the basals and also a proliferation of supplementary phonics workbooks, kits, and games for home and the classroom. The pendulum had started swinging in the direction of phonics.

Other challenges to the conventional wisdom of the basals emerged in the 1960s, which became known as a decade of innovations in teaching reading (Chall, 1967; Robinson, 1968; Vilscek, 1968). Besides intensive phonics, other alternatives were:

- *Language experience.* This approach was a descendant of the *reading to words and letters* approach as conceived by Francis Parker and others. In this approach, students' oral language is transcribed and used as materials for reading, writing, speaking, and listening. Immersion in all forms of language is central.
- *Individualized reading.* An alternative to basal programs, this approach emphasizes student self-selection of reading materials, usually from a classroom library of children's books, and self-pacing in reading progress. The teacher holds individual con-

ferences with students regularly for teaching, evaluation, and small-group work.

• *Modified alphabets.* These approaches used additional alphabet characters and diacritical marks to increase the correspondence between the 26 traditional English letters and the approximately 44 speech sounds used in English. The modified alphabet method was used in special beginning reading books that gradually phased into the traditional alphabet. The Initial Teaching Alphabet (i.t.a.) was the most accepted modified alphabet in the United States and Great Britain.

• *Programmed reading.* Programmed reading is instruction in which the reading task is broken into very small parts to which the reader responds in sequence (hundreds in an hour) and gets immediate feedback on the correctness of the response. This approach soon evolved into reading "management systems" using hundreds of subskill units with frequent criterion-referenced testing. Programmed materials were originally in workbook form, but later became computerized.

• *Linguistic approaches.* These approaches exposed beginning readers to easily decodable words grouped into word families such as *-at* (*fat, cat, sat, mat,* etc.). The use of highly regular sound–symbol patterns in words in simple sentences (*The fat cat sat on a mat*) was advocated by some linguists of the day (Fries, 1962), although this practice could be traced back to the McGuffey readers and before.

While many such alternatives were introduced in the 1960s, the basals clearly held favor in a large majority of classrooms. Many of the new techniques were used as supplements to the basals or as alternative methods for students who were progressing slowly or experiencing difficulty.

The concern for more intense phonics and the other alternatives resulted in what Chall (1967) called "the great debate" over how best to teach beginning reading. She referred to the two opposing approaches as *code emphasis* (phonics first) and *meaning em-*

phasis (sight words first). As we have seen, this debate in various forms dated back well more than 100 years. Chall reviewed the research literature on this issue and bemoaned the poor quality of much of it. She cautiously took the position that early emphasis on phonics and decoding was more effective than using a conventional basal series that focused on sight vocabulary and reading for meaning. However, whereas Chall's code emphasis position became popular and influential, her conclusions were not as well supported as is sometimes assumed.

During the period 1964–1965, the U.S. Office of Education (USOE) supported 27 coordinated studies comparing different methods of teaching first-grade reading. All of the alternatives noted earlier were included. Each alternative was compared with the basal reader method in several different school locations. Of these 27 studies, 13 were continued through the second grade, and eight followed their students through third grade. Unfortunately, differences in the way the studies were conducted at each location made direct comparisons impossible. At the end of the first year, a comparison of results on several reading measures was inconclusive because the superiority of one method or another on one measure or another differed by location, with most differences being insignificant. Children learned to read, or failed to learn to read, in each method, and particulars of location such as teacher and school seemed to make more difference than the method itself. The second-grade and third-grade follow-up studies found the same general pattern. Thus, the largest scale controlled studies ever done in the United States indicated no consistent advantage for any method when participants were followed through the third grade. Even in referring to the first-grade results alone, the researchers concluded that no one method was so outstanding that it should be used to the exclusion of others (Bond & Dykstra, 1967). Similar conclusions were soon drawn in Great Britain (Department of Education and Science, 1975).

The USOE had also commissioned the Educational Testing Service to do a comprehensive review of the existing research literature on the status of reading and its teaching. Using several criteria for evaluating research quality, the final results of that review (Corder, 1971) did not concur with Chall's (1967) conclusions about methods. Of 612 research studies comparing methods that were reviewed, only 265 (43%) met Corder's criteria for adequate reliability and validity. The studies reviewed included the USOE first-grade studies and their follow-up studies as well as other published studies. Comparison showed that different methods of teaching reading did *not* produce significantly different results. Although more comprehensive and rigorous, this review did not gain the celebrity that Chall's review did, possibly because the results did not allow for taking a strong position. We will return to Corder's review in Chapter 7.

THE LATER 20TH CENTURY

The scene in the early 1970s was dominated by basals that had grown into complete reading curricula encompassing more phonics, a more systematic approach to introducing and reinforcing reading skills of all kinds, and numerous ancillaries including tests, duplicating masters, supplementary reading books for individualized reading, and so on. Empirical studies of differences in the content of major basal programs showed that they were remarkably alike (Goodman & Page, 1978; Sadoski, 1982). Reading had become big business, and the competitive efforts of publishers to provide all-inclusive programs prescribed the teaching–learning situation as never before. However, more fundamental changes were brewing.

The emerging sciences of linguistics and cognitive psychology, and their intersection, psycholinguistics, began to impact our knowledge of reading with implications for its teaching. The psycholinguistic reading theories of Kenneth Goodman, Frank Smith, and others brought a change to the scene starting in the 1970s that would become known as *whole language*. This holistic approach was a view of reading that combined new trends in linguistics and cognitive psychology with the earlier progressive education ideas of Parker, Dewey, and others. It was the latest incarnation of the *reading to words and letters* approach. Perhaps its closest predecessor was the language experience approach.

These psycholinguistic reading theories maintained that the subsystems of reading, including sound–symbol correspondences, grammar, and semantics, constantly interacted as readers made sense of text and constructed meaning. Hence, reading should always occur in a full communicative context (i.e., whole), not as isolated sounds, letters, or words devoid of realistic context. The new curriculum reflected these theoretical principles, much as the basals had reflected the theories of Gray. From the start, children should be surrounded by environmental print (e.g., signs, labels) and read authentic children's literature suitable for beginners. The latter characteristic was not dissimilar to the movement toward using real literature in beginning reading seen around the turn of the century. As reading progressed, the focus was to stay always on comprehension and meaning. Writing was also much a part of the curriculum, and the integration of all the language arts across the curriculum was central.

The holistic approach opposed intensive phonics and skills-oriented basals with controlled vocabulary that stressed decoding first. The differences between the skills approach and the holistic approach is discussed throughout this book, so we will not detail those differences here. However, this movement started the historical pendulum swinging once again, this time away from phonics and decoding and toward comprehension and response in teaching reading.

The holistic approach attracted the interest of many reading educators. But despite growing professional and public interest during the 1970s and 1980s, the basal readers still remained the most popular teaching materials during this time, often supplemented with more phonics, on the one hand, and more children's literature and writing, on the other (e.g., Cloud-Silva & Sadoski,

1987). This situation could alternately be interpreted as either (1) a profession that had become overreliant on commercial programs, or (2) an effort to seek balance by teachers who saw numerous options and wanted to expose students to many of them. Furthermore, there was resistance to whole language from some teachers, linguists, and psychologists.

As the 20th century drew to a close, the pendulum would swing back toward decoding. In 1990, Marilyn Jager Adams published *Beginning to Read*, an influential book that recommended more balance between whole language and phonics. In particular, the book stressed "phonemic awareness," the ability of children to tell sounds apart in spoken words, as an important precursor of learning phonics. Interest among researchers, educators, and the public during the 1990s was heavily centered on developing phonemic awareness and decoding, and the overall popularity of the holistic approach began to wane. Although much controversy remained, the close of the 20th century found a growing trend toward balance in teaching reading. A national survey in 1998 indicated that 89% of elementary teachers agreed with the statement "I believe in a balanced approach to reading instruction which combines skills development with literature and language-rich activities" (Baumann, Hoffman, Moon, & Duffy-Hester, 1998). Much of the rest of this book explores this trend.

CONCLUSION

As noted in Chapter 1, the emergence of two opposing positions and efforts to find an appropriate balance are not unique to the United States or other English-speaking countries (Downing, 1973). The extremes of this continuum have been debated around the world for many years and will likely continue to be debated far into the future. In political fashion, approaches and methods have leaned toward one extreme or the other, and often have attempted compromises on some middle ground.

Despite the fact that research and practice have largely failed to identify one clear and unambiguous recipe for teaching reading, historical arguments are not without merit. The historical argument against decoding-emphasis approaches is that they produce readers who are mechanically proficient but pay too little attention to meaning. The historical argument against comprehension-emphasis approaches is that they produce readers who lack independence in reading unfamiliar text. However, few would disagree that mature readers lacking either ability are at a disadvantage. The truth may well be that different methods or combinations of methods work better for *some* students in *some* situations than others.

REFERENCES

Adams, M. J. (1990). *Beginning to read: Thinking and learning about print.* Cambridge, MA: MIT Press.

Baumann, J. F., Hoffman, J. V., Moon, J., & Duffy-Hester, A. M. (1998). Where are teachers' voices in the phonics/whole language debate?: Results from a survey of U.S. elementary classroom teachers. *The Reading Teacher, 51,* 636–650.

Bond, G. L., & Dykstra, R. (1967). The cooperative research program in first grade reading instruction. *Reading Research Quarterly, 2,* 5–142.

Chall, J. S. (1967). *Learning to read: The great debate.* New York: McGraw-Hill.

Cloud-Silva, C., & Sadoski, M. (1987). Reading teachers' attitudes toward basal reader use and state adoption policies. *Journal of Educational Research, 81,* 5–16.

Corder, R. (1971). *The information base for reading: A critical review of the information base for current assumptions regarding the status of instruction and achievement in the United States.* Educational Testing Service, U.S. Office of Education Project 0-9031, Final Report. (ERIC Document Reproduction Service No. ED 054 922)

Department of Education and Science. (1975). *A language for life (the Bullock report).* London: Her Majesty's Stationers Office.

Downing, J. (1973). *Comparative reading: Cross-national studies of behavior and processes in reading and writing.* New York: Macmillan.

Flesch, R. (1955). *Why Johnny can't read and what you can do about it.* New York: Harper.

Fries, C. C. (1962). *Linguistics and reading.* New York: Holt, Rinehart & Winston.

Goodman, K. S., & Page, W. D. (1978). *Reading comprehension programs: Theoretical bases of reading instruction in the middle grades.* National Institute of Education, U. S. Department of Health, Education, and Welfare, Revised Final Report. (ERIC Document Reproduction Service No. ED 165 092)

Gray, W. S., Artley, A. S., & Arbuthnot, M. H. (1951). *The new we look and see.* The New Basic Readers Curriculum Foundation Series. Chicago: Scott, Foresman.

Huey, E. B. (1908). *The psychology and pedagogy of reading.* New York: Macmillan. (Reprinted 1968, Cambridge, MA: MIT Press)

Laing, M. E. (1903). *Reading: A manual for teachers.* Boston: Heath.

Mathews, M. M. (1966). *Teaching to read: Historically considered.* Chicago: University of Chicago Press.

McGuffey's First Eclectic Reader (rev. ed.). (1879). Van Antwerp, Bragg & Co. (Reprinted 1997, Hoboken, NJ: Wiley, 1997)

Norton, D. E. (2003). *Through the eyes of a child: An introduction to children's literature* (6th ed.). Upper Saddle River, NJ: Merrill/Prentice-Hall.

Parker, F. W. (1894/1969). *Talks on pedagogics.* New York: Arno Press.

Robinson, H. M. (Ed.). (1968). *Innovation and change in reading instruction* (67th yearbook of the National Society for the Study of Education). Chicago: University of Chicago Press.

Sadoski, M. (1982). *A study of the theoretical bases of reading instruction and a comparison of programs.* Texas A&M University Instructional Research Laboratory Technical Paper No. R83001. (ERIC Document Reproduction Service No. ED 236 543)

Sadoski, M., & Paivio, A. (2001). *Imagery and text: A dual coding theory of reading and writing.* Mahwah, NJ: Erlbaum.

Smith, N. B. (2002). *American reading instruction* (special ed.). Newark, DE: International Reading Association.

Vilscek, E. C. (Ed.). (1968). *A decade of innovations: Approaches to beginning reading.* Newark, DE: International Reading Association.

CHAPTER 3

Why?

The Goals of Teaching Reading

Reading textbooks typically discuss many aspects of reading: the scope and sequence of the reading curriculum, or the *what* to teach in reading; the methods and materials of reading, or the *how* to teach reading; and evaluation, the *how well* of teaching reading. All these topics are discussed in this book. But the one topic seldom mentioned is the goals, or the *why* of teaching reading. This chapter lays out a balanced set of goals for the teaching of reading.

The goals of teaching any subject can be derived and organized from broad taxonomies of learning. Such taxonomies, or systems of classification, have been developed over many years and applied in many fields of education, including certain aspects of reading (e.g., Pearson & Johnson, 1978; Smith & Barrett, 1979). Bloom and his coworkers (Bloom, Engelhart, Furst, Hill, & Krathwohl, 1956; Bloom, 1994; Krathwohl, Bloom, & Masia, 1964) developed an influential and enduring taxonomy of general educational objectives.

According to this taxonomy, anything that can be taught and learned is classified in one or more of three great domains:

- The psychomotor domain
- The affective domain
- The cognitive domain

The *psychomotor domain* is the domain of the mind and the body working together to produce physical performances. There is a great range of skill in psychomotor performances from tasks involving basic locomotive and manipulative acts to highly creative physical performances. Learning to walk, tie shoelaces, swim, type, drive a car, and perform creative dance routines are examples of psychomotor activities.

The *affective domain* is the domain of attitudes, interests, values, appreciation, and life adjustment. Affective behaviors vary from simple selective attention through the development of an internally consistent character structure. Responding positively to success and constructively to failure, adopting healthy habits over unhealthy ones, developing a democratic tolerance for opposing points of view, or invoking ethical principles for behavior in morally ambiguous situations are common examples of affective activities.

The *cognitive domain* is the domain of intellectual skill including the recall or recognition of information, the comprehension of information, and the development of logical and rational thought skills such as analysis, synthesis, and evaluation. Remembering facts, summarizing thoughts, applying principles to solve problems, deducing a coherent explanation from disparate pieces of evidence, or objectively critiquing arguments in terms of their logical consistency are common examples of cognitive activities.

Educational theorists are quick to point out that the separation of the domains is somewhat artificial and that learning often occurs in a way that involves more than one domain. Our actions, attitudes, and intellectual abilities are all related in complex ways. Discussions of the relationship between cognitive and affective development, in particular, sometimes sound like the chicken-or-the-egg argument. Some maintain that positive attitudes toward a subject come from knowledge of that subject, whereas others maintain that motivation for a subject leads to gaining more knowledge about it. Whatever the truth of these positions, taxonomies have long proven useful for organizing, teaching, and testing subject matter in schools.

APPLYING THE TAXONOMY
TO TEACHING READING

This three-domain taxonomy of learning can be effectively applied to the goals of teaching reading. An efficient result of this application is to reduce the goal domains to two by eliminating the psychomotor domain.

As a largely sedentary activity, reading involves few psychomotor acts. We move our eyes across lines of text. We may occasionally use a finger to keep our place. We turn pages in books or scroll text on computer screens. We may use speech articulation to read aloud or subvocalize as we read. Beyond this, little psychomotor activity is involved in reading, and most of this activity is not specifically taught. We can therefore safely omit the teaching of psychomotor skills from our goals in the general teaching of reading.

Take note that psychomotor skill training *does* occur in teaching reading, but it is mainly relegated to learning special skills in special situations. For example, speed-reading courses involve lessons in eye movements to increase the visual perceptual span, lessons in hand motions that sweep across and down pages to propel the reader forward, and even efficient page-turning techniques to increase speed. For another example, remedial reading or special education courses may involve multisensory learning techniques such as training in speech articulation, learning letters through touch and feel as well as sight, and even physically acting out sentence meanings to demonstrate comprehension.

However, the focus of this book is the general classroom and the typical student. The affective domain and the cognitive domain are of primary interest. We will return to these domains after some additional exploration of the purposes pursued in reading.

STUDIES OF WHY PEOPLE READ

Several conceptual analyses and empirical studies have refined our knowledge of why people read. Guthrie and Greany (1991, p. 89) conceptually analyzed the literacy activities of adults and presented the following summary classifications:

> The uses, functions, and purposes for adult literacy may be conceptualized as knowledge gain, participation in society, personal empowerment, and occupational effectiveness. Searching brief documents is mandatory for competence in the workplace and participation in societal groups and organizations. Reading fiction and literature seems to enhance the sense of enjoyment and empowerment of individuals. Reading articles on news, science, and contemporary problems enhances the information level of individuals.

Greany and Neuman (1990) empirically studied children's reasons for reading through questionnaires administered in 15 countries to thousands of 10- and 13-year-old students. They found three underlying factors that they termed "utility," "enjoyment," and "escape." *Utility* was reading to learn to become successful in school or life, *enjoyment* was reading for pleasure and interest, and *escape* was reading to kill time or avoid boredom.

Clear similarities exist between adults' reasons for reading and children's reasons for reading in the two studies. Both include a goal related to reading to gain knowledge for successful participation in literacy activities at school or at work (cognitive emphasis).

46

Both include one or more goals related to pursuing interests and enjoyment (affective emphasis). In sum, these goals closely resemble the cognitive and affective domains discussed earlier. These studies of the purposes for reading provide a degree of validity for using these two domains as the basis of a set of goals for teaching reading.

GOALS OF TEACHING READING

The goals of teaching reading offered here will be balanced between the affective domain and the cognitive domain. Similar cognitive and affective goals have been suggested by Walmsley (1981), Mosenthal (1987), and Gates (1951/2002), among others. The goal statements below are consistent with other treatments of the subject but are new as offered here.

Affective Goals

Two goals in the affective domain need to be addressed in the teaching of reading. They can be distinguished by the conceptual difference between *attitudes* and *interests*.

Goal 1: Developing Positive Attitudes toward Reading

Children and adults who are developing reading ability need to approach reading acts positively and gain some confidence in their competency to perform those acts. The term *attitude*, as used here, applies to readers' perceptions of their competence and their disposition toward their future performance. Beginners at any complex activity often experience difficulty and frustration. The reader may remember his or her early efforts to play the piano, hit a baseball, solve mathematics problems, or accomplish some other activity requiring new knowledge and skill, and how at first he or she felt hopelessly incompetent ("I'll never get this!"). Early failures can breed defeatist attitudes, while early successes bolster confidence.

The development of a positive attitude toward reading means progressing in our confidence in our own ability as a reader. Ideally, students should experience success regularly and approach reading confidently, with a "can do" spirit, rather than avoiding it because it is painful and frustrating. People seldom continue willingly to do that which causes them pain. Moreover, educators are not in the business of seeing how much pain they can inflict on their students. Several characterizations might make this point more clear:

Characterizes positive attitude	Characterizes negative attitude
success	failure
confidence	insecurity
satisfaction	frustration
acceptance	stigmatization
self-esteem	shame

Readers who experienced difficulty with reading and who were banished to the lowest reading group in school can attest to the negative attitude that so often accompanies early failure and stigmatization. Learning to read is not simple; it is particularly vexing for some, and it is hard work for nearly everyone. Few fledgling readers experience immediate and total success, but ideally none should be allowed to develop a seriously negative mind-set toward reading.

Experiencing success is important in early reading, but the development of positive attitudes reappears as a goal every time a reader is exposed to a new subject with its own vocabulary, symbol system, or discourse structures. Reading stories is not the same as reading science, mathematics, documents, maps, or computer languages. Every field, it seems, has its own jargon and text conventions that can be confusing to the uninitiated. A quick look in the appendices of a dictionary will display a bewildering array of special signs and symbols such as those used in astronomy, biology, chemistry, electricity, finance, linguistics, mathematics, or medicine, to name just a few. Specialized maps such as weather charts or geographical projections are often cryptic until their readers master their legends. Readers in the middle or upper grades and even adults need assistance and patience in dealing with these new systems much as beginners do. In fact, they are beginners, only at a higher level.

Goal 2: Developing Personal Interests and Tastes in Reading

Readers are not just people who *can* read, they are people who *do* read. Just as a surfer is not someone who can surf, but someone who does surf, and just as a golfer is not someone who can play golf, but someone who does play golf, so it goes with reading. Having a positive attitude is not enough. Lifelong readers choose to pursue their life interests through reading, at least in part, and in doing so they develop value judgments about what they read. A second goal in the affective domain is the development of personal interests and discriminating tastes.

Attitude is typically distinguished from interest in reading (e.g., Guthrie & Greany, 1991; Taylor, Harris, Pearson, & Garcia, 1995). Interest builds upon a positive attitude but goes beyond it. Readers who can read competently and who know that they can learn to read better sometimes are simply not interested in reading and do not pursue their interests through reading. Stated differently, reaching Goal 1 is a necessary but not a sufficient condition for reaching Goal 2.

The distinction between having a positive attitude toward reading (Goal 1) and a personal interest in reading (Goal 2) is captured in the word *aliteracy*. An aliterate individual is not illiterate; the illiterate person cannot read. The aliterate person can read but doesn't. The aliterate reader has the ability but not the motivation, and therefore doesn't develop fully as a reader and perhaps not as a person.

Having an interest in reading means having the motivation to read and to respond affectively, to seek to enlarge our self-understanding and our sense of self-worth through reading. Reading about a subject is a common part of being interested in that subject even if the subject is not an inherently verbal one. Internet sites devoted to written discussion on virtually any subject proliferate. A quick scan of the magazine section in a supermarket reveals common periodicals on a broad array of interests: current events and politics, entertainment and celebrities, travel and leisure, hobbies and sports, clothing and fashion, and so on. Contemporary bookstores offer lounge chairs and designer coffee. Some bookstores are devoted entirely to children's literature. There is even a Book TV network. All these are the surface evidence of our desire to pursue life interests through reading, to grow and respond more fully through reading.

Beyond the development of interest is the development of discriminating value judgment, or taste. The terms *discriminating* and *taste* are not used in any elitist sense here. Rather, they refer to the tendency of interested readers to make value choices and judgments about what they chose to read and to develop their own critical standards. While we may not all agree on what book or author is preferable, we should have preferences and our own reasons for having them. Reading a tightly argued, factual, and logical editorial persuades us more than a blatant emotional appeal even if we tend to agree with the position of the latter. After reading enough pulp romance novels, the adolescent may tend to seek the appeal of a classic romance like *Jane Eyre* or *Pride and Prejudice*. Literary scholar Clifton Fadiman in *The New Lifetime Reading Plan* (Fadiman & Major, 1997, p. xx) writes that you should read quality literature, both fiction and nonfiction, "to change your interior life into something a little more interesting, as a love affair does, or some task calling upon your deepest energies." The literary critic Harold Bloom (2001, p. 22), in his best-seller *How to Read and Why*, suggests that reading great literature is really the pursuit of affective virtue: "Ultimately we read—as Bacon, Johnson, and Emerson agree—in order to strengthen the self, and to learn its authentic interests." For the serious absorbed reader in any field, the pursuit of the difficult pleasure of reading borders on passion. In June 2003, the recently released, 870-page fifth book of the Harry Potter series was selling at the rate of eight copies a second!

Cognitive Goals

Two goals in the cognitive domain cover the utilitarian aspects of reading and the development of the mental skills that allow us to continue to mature as readers for the rest of our lives. Since the second of these goals requires considerable elaboration, a subsequent chapter is partly devoted to it.

Goal 3: Developing the Use of Reading as a Tool to Solve Problems

Reading weighs heavily in the tool belt of a working, technological society. It helps us to solve a broad array of personal and social problems in a complex, literate world. Try to imagine a day without reading anything. Print is everywhere: memos and menus, candy wrappers and constitutions, bills and bumper stickers, cereal boxes and serial numbers, obituaries and optical charts, resumes and rest room doors. One has to travel to completely undeveloped areas or to the wilderness to avoid encountering printed language in some form. And even there we would carry it on our clothing!

Reading is a way to navigate in a literate realm. Reading helps us to get from point A to point B, whether these points are as close as connected websites on the Internet or as far as the journey from ignorant obscurity to educated influence. The illiterate or functionally illiterate live in a very limited world, closed off from much participation in society, limited in their compass of opportunities for employment or advancement. Ideally, readers should be able to apply the broadest scope of reading procedures to the broadest scope of materials and social situations where reading tasks are found, whether at home or at work, whether for citizenship or for recreation.

Reading is a way to deal with everyday problems where printed language is a feasible or requisite solution. Such problems embrace a broad array of everyday tasks and materials from reading food packaging for the proper setting for microwaving a frozen meal to completing job applications and income tax forms. The largest part of our reading is not recreational, but school-related (reading to learn) or work-related (reading to do). Literacy instruction is a legal requirement in public, private, or home schools, and the use of textbooks in teaching school subjects is virtually universal. Mikulecky and Drew (1991) found that most U.S. adults read and write more in the workplace than they do anywhere else—time in the workplace spent reading print, charts, graphs, and computer text averaged about 2 hours a day. Only 2% of the wide variety of professions they examined required no reading or writing, and they found an increasing demand for job literacy with few exceptions. Clearly, using reading as a tool in our daily lives is pervasive.

Two aspects of using reading as a tool to address large-scale social problems can be summarized. One aspect is educational reading. One mission of education is to transmit the knowledge base of civilization to new generations along with the capability to increase that knowledge base and improve life. Academic journals in all fields of endeavor present new findings for critical review and archive those findings. This accumulated knowledge, interpreted and reinterpreted, has led to progress on every scientific front. Also, the traditions, values, truths, myths, and legends of different cultures and religions are preserved and passed on through educational texts. This aspect of utilitarian reading may be seen as conservative—conserving the accumulated knowledge and wisdom of a culture and transmitting it.

Another aspect of the utilitarian goal of reading is emancipation. Literacy is a means to liberate the mind and the spirit. Reading can free individuals or societies from oppression and dogma.

Writers with different sociopolitical and religious views express those views extensively in free societies, and these words eventually find their way to oppressed societies. It may be naïve to believe that the written word alone can eliminate oppression, but the dictum that the pen is mightier than the sword has often proven true throughout history. This aspect of utilitarian reading can be seen as liberal—to challenge and change established conventions.

Goal 4: Developing the Fundamental Competencies of Reading at Succeedingly Higher Levels of Independence

Developing the fundamental competencies that comprise reading is the most basic goal and requires more extensive discussion. Therefore, we discuss only the second part of this goal statement here and deal with the first part in the next chapter.

This goal provides the means to the other ends. When the fundamental competencies of reading have been taught and learned, the reader is equipped to pursue reading as a continuing, lifelong endeavor. These competencies are learned to some extent in succeeding stages. Chall (1996) proposed six stages of reading:

- Stage 0, Prereading (prekindergarten–grade 1)—developing concepts about print; recognizing print in the environment; learning some letters and words.
- Stage 1, Initial Reading or Decoding (grades 1–2)—learning letters and letter combinations and their correspondence with parts of spoken words; learning to crack the code.
- Stage 2, Confirmation, Fluency, Ungluing from Print (grades 2–3)—learning more about decoding; using context to increase fluency and rate; reading simple stories and beginners' books.
- Stage 3, Reading for Learning the New: A First Step (grades 4–8)—learning to read begins to shift to reading to learn;

developing vocabulary and knowledge; beginning to use subject area textbooks.

- Stage 4, Multiple Viewpoints (high school)—dealing with more mature texts that introduce varying viewpoints and more challenging concepts; more independent reading.
- Stage 5, Construction and Reconstruction—A World View (college and adult)—more advanced and discriminating reading; constructing knowledge on a high level of abstraction and generality; varying purposes and rate; critical reading.

Acceptance of Chall's "ages and stages" is not universal. However, these stages are a reasonable conceptual description of the way reading has been traditionally taught and learned, and the stages reflect a gradual shift from learning to read to reading to learn. The development of all the fundamentals of reading is covered in these stages, gradually building mature readers who can continue to read and learn on their own. The end result is readers who are no longer dependent on schools or teachers, readers who can read and respond independently for the rest of their lives.

Expressed differently, we expect middle-grade students to independently read more text and more difficult text than students in the primary grades; we expect high school students to independently read more text and more difficult text than students in the middle grades; and we expect college students to independently read more text and more difficult text than high school students. Students at each succeeding level are expected to become more independent at reading in all its basic forms. Ultimately, the goal is to produce a citizenry capable of self-education to any level needed or desired.

This does not mean that anyone with a high school or college education can take any book on any subject, regardless of how advanced, and comprehend it independently. This depends on more than reading. Life experience, motivation, and opportunity play their roles. But after these factors are considered, reading ability should not be an impediment to any quest for knowledge involving reading. Reference works can be consulted, or easier, introductory books can be digested first. To truly grow in and through reading, we must pull ourselves up by the bootstraps, work our way up to books that are at first beyond us.

The goal of independence in reading is more than academic. This goal is critical to the growth of a democratic society with a citizenry that can become informed for themselves rather than depending on press releases or canned commentary. It is critical to experiencing the life of the mind and the life of the heart in all their richness; to grow in understanding, feeling, and wisdom; to truly become all that we have the right to become. Reading teachers are truly important people.

The next chapter elaborates on the fundamental competencies of reading to complete our explanation of this goal. However, we end this chapter with two summary propositions:

1. Any general reading curriculum that met the four goals defined here would be achieving something close to ideal. Few authorities in reading would cavil with a curriculum that met these goals, whatever reasonable teaching methods it employed. Ideal situations in any field are hard to envision (and harder to accomplish), but this balanced set of goals summarizes an idealized and attainable scenario. Taken together, the goals help us to imagine an ideal state of affairs in a reading class and provide a conceptual basis for the *why* of teaching reading.

2. Conversely, any reading curriculum that does not at least address these four goals is necessarily incomplete. A complete reading curriculum needs to address the affective as well as the cognitive, attitude as well as ability, interest as well as skill. In fact, aliteracy may be one of our most pressing literacy issues, because with reading, as with other abilities, its value lies not in its possession but in its use. But conversely, it is not sufficient to have motivated readers who read with little skill or read only in a restricted

domain such as simple fiction. The philosopher's "golden mean" seems to apply well to curriculum design in reading.

REFERENCES

Bloom, B. S. (1994). Reflections on the development and use of the taxonomy. In L. W. Anderson & L. A. Sosniak (Eds.), *Bloom's taxonomy: A forty-year retrospective* (93rd yearbook of the National Society for the Study of Education, pp. 1–8). Chicago: University of Chicago Press.

Bloom, B. S., Engelhart, M. D., Furst, E. J., Hill, W. H., & Krathwohl, D. R. (1956). *Taxonomy of educational objectives. Handbook I: Cognitive domain.* New York: McKay.

Bloom, H. (2000). *How to read and why.* New York: Simon & Schuster.

Chall, J. S. (1996). *Stages of reading development* (2nd ed.). Fort Worth, TX: Harcourt Brace College Publishers.

Fadiman, C., & Major, J. S. (1997). *The new lifetime reading plan* (4th ed.). New York: Harper Collins.

Gates, A. I. (1951/2002). What should we teach in reading? *School and Community, 36,* 13–14. (Reprinted in *Reading Psychology, 23,* 341–344.

Greaney, V., & Neuman, S. B. (1990). The functions of reading: A cross-cultural perspective. *Reading Research Quarterly, 25,* 173–195.

Guthrie, J. T., & Greaney, V. (1991). Literacy acts. In R. Barr, M. L. Kamil, P. B. Mosenthal, & P. D. Pearson (Eds.), *Handbook of reading research* (Vol. II, pp. 68–96). White Plains, NY: Longman.

Krathwohl, D. R., Bloom, B. S., & Masia, B. B. (1964). *Taxonomy of educational objectives: The classification of educational goals. Handbook II: Affective domain.* New York: McKay.

Mikulecky, L., & Drew, R. (1991). Basic literacy skills in the workplace. In R. Barr, M. L. Kamil, P. B. Mosenthal, & P. D. Pearson (Eds.), *Handbook of reading research* (Vol. II, pp. 669–689). White Plains, NY: Longman.

Mosenthal, P. B. (1987). The goals of reading research and practice: Making sense of the many means of reading. *The Reading Teacher, 40,* 694–699.

Pearson, P. D., & Johnson, D. D. (1978). *Teaching reading comprehension*. New York: Holt, Rinehart, & Winston.

Smith, R. J., & Barrett, T. C. (1979). *Teaching reading in the middle grades* (2nd ed.). Reading, MA: Addison-Wesley.

Taylor, B., Harris, L. A., Pearson, P. D., & Garcia, G. (1995). *Reading difficulties: Instruction and assessment* (2nd ed.). New York: McGraw-Hill.

Walmsely, S. A. (1981). On the purpose and content of secondary reading programs: An educational ideological perspective. *Curriculum Inquiry, 11*, 73–93.

CHAPTER 4

What?

The Fundamental Competencies of Reading

This chapter completes our explanation from the previous chapter of the last and most basic goal of teaching reading: Developing the fundamental competencies of reading at succeedingly higher levels of independence. By "fundamental competencies" we mean the basic, underlying abilities without which reading printed language could not be fully accomplished. These are the competencies at which we expect individuals to become succeedingly more skilled and independent as they grow as readers.

Although the list of competencies presented here may appear simple, their underlying perceptual, cognitive, and linguistic processes are much more complex and still not completely understood. This problem, however, is in the realm of reading theory, and our concern is with a conceptual framework that is useful for teaching reading.

This is not to imply that the conceptual framework presented here is superficial, however. In fact, it is philosophical. *Linguistic philosophy* is that branch of metaphysics that explains what we mean by our words. The linguistic philosopher Gilbert Ryle in his book *The Concept of Mind* (1949) argued that the mind is a set of capacities and abilities that can be categorized as *knowing that* or *knowing how*. Reading is of the knowing how category, and it has been in turn philosophically categorized. L. B. Daniels (1970, 1980, 1982) categorized reading into three capacities or abilities: *reading as saying, reading as understanding,* and *reading as (reflective) thinking.* That conceptual stratification is similar to the fundamental competencies discussed here and was one of the bases for their original proposal (Sadoski, 1982). We will refer to these three fundamental competencies in the contemporary parlance of reading as *decoding, comprehension,* and *response.*

DECODING

The term *decoding* as used in reading is unfortunately imprecise. In general language, decoding implies understanding (e.g., to decode a message). In reading, the term generally means converting printed language to spoken language whether it is understood or not, and whether it is converted to overt, oral speech or to covert, inner speech. In decoding, we produce the spoken analog of the printed language but not *necessarily* the thought analog. The term *decoding* will be used in that sense here.

A more preferable term for some is *recoding,* implying only that the code has changed from the orthographic, print code to the phonological, speech code. We can, for example, do a fair job at recoding printed languages that we do not understand well or at all: *No entiendo esta escritura* ("I don't understand this writing" in Spanish). We can probably produce a fairly accurate spoken analog of this sentence even if we don't know its meaning. We will use the term *decoding* to refer to this situation as well as to situations where at least some meaning is understood.

Even if we speak the language we are decoding, understanding may be distant. Consider how we would read an insurance policy, a legal document, or any text on a subject of which we know little or nothing, even if it is written in English. We may read it fluently in the sense of pronouncing the words in order with appropriate sentence intonations, but we would probably grasp little or none of the meaning ("It's Greek to me"). We could agree, however, that we were "reading." This is another example of reading as decoding without necessarily understanding.

One thing readers learn to do when they learn to decode in this sense is to pronounce printed words. Decoding at the word level is called *word recognition*. This term simply means figuring out how a printed word is most likely to be pronounced whether or not we are familiar with that pronunciation and whether or not we know what it means. The term *word identification* is sometimes used synonymously, but it generally also implies assigning a meaning as well as a pronunciation to a printed word (i.e., decoding the message). This distinction is necessary because it is possible to determine the spoken form of printed words without understanding their meaning, as noted. On the other hand, it is possible to understand a printed word's meaning without necessarily providing a correct pronunciation or any pronunciation if the context is strong enough. Consider the word *Oswiecim* in the sentence *Oswiecim is the Polish name for Auschwitz*. The reader unfamiliar with Polish might not supply the correct pronunciation (Osh-vyan-tsim) but would still grasp the meaning. Comprehension does not invariably require decoding.

Decoding may apply to printed units smaller than words, such as letters or letter combinations that form common syllables or morphemes (units of meaning such as prefixes, suffixes, or roots of words). Typically a part of "sounding out" words, this competency is used by readers at all levels. Consider the chemical name *alkylbenzyldimethylammonium*. In decoding this word, you probably analyzed it (broke it down) into pronounceable letter combinations, and synthesized them (put them together) into an approximate or final pronunciation. The units may have been of different sizes, with larger, more familiar units such as *ammonium* possibly recognized as wholes, and even understood as morphemes.

The usual tendency is to decode units of the largest possible size, so that familiar letter combinations such as *al* are recognized rather than *a* and *l* separately. This is why words became divided between syllables when they extend from one printed line to another—the decoding process is expected to occur at the syllable level at least. In some situations, we may be reduced to letter-by-letter decoding, but these situations are found only in extreme cases and may not be successful.

Decoding can be achieved in several ways, which form the basis of most of its teaching. These ways are:

- Phonics
- Structural analysis
- Sight vocabulary
- Context
- Dictionary

Phonics

Phonics is the way, just introduced, to "sound it out" at the level of individual letters or simple letter combinations. The basis of phonics is our accumulated knowledge about the way *graphemes* stand for *phonemes*. A *grapheme* is the smallest unit in a written language, a letter of the alphabet in alphabetic languages. We have 26 letters in English. A *phoneme* is the smallest unit in a spoken language. We have approximately 44 phonemes in English, although there is some disagreement about the number. Written languages are a way to represent their corresponding spoken languages; the way the printed form maps onto the spoken form is the basis of phonics. For example, the word *fine* is distinguished from the "word" *kine* by the difference in the initial phoneme and corresponding grapheme. In fact, the word *kine* is an archaic word meaning cows, but readers should be able to decode this word even if they are unfamiliar with its meaning. We use phonics to aid word recognition this way.

This system in English is unfortunately not a matter of one-to-one correspondences, as can be readily inferred from the mismatch between 26 graphemes and 44 phonemes (other languages, such as Turkish and Finnish, have much closer correspondence). This is complicated by the fact that graphemes can stand for more than one phoneme (*c* represents different phonemes in *cow*, *city*, *cello*, etc.), and phonemes can be represented by different graphemes (the /f/ phoneme is represented by *f* in *fine*, *ph* in *phone*, *gh* in *rough*, etc.). Also, notice the unpronounced or "silent" *e* at the end of *fine*, *kine*, *phone*, and many other words. Some letters, particularly some consonants, are highly reliable in their correspondence with speech sounds in English, while others, especially vowels, are less reliable. Both vowels and consonants are unpronounced in many words.

Two main kinds of phonics are synthetic phonics and analytic phonics. *Synthetic phonics* is part-to-whole and involves associating individual graphemes with individual phonemes, blending sets of them into words, and learning generalizations that govern the allowable sets. *Analytic phonics* is whole-to-part and involves learning a number of words and their related phonic generalizations, which are then applied to still other words. Phonics is a complex, imperfect system and some of it is seldom if ever taught, but readers develop considerable phonics knowledge whether they are taught it or pick it up on their own.

Structural Analysis

Words can be broken down into units larger than individual graphemes and phonemes, as seen earlier. We probably perceive the largest familiar units for the sake of efficiency, but in any case structures larger than letters but smaller than words are commonly perceived and used in decoding. This is the basis of structural analysis.

Words can be seen as having two kinds of structure: sound structure and meaning structure. The main sound structures are *syllables*, units of spoken language with a single vowel sound and usually consonant sounds as well. Every word has at least one syllable but may have more. The *al* in *alkyl* is a syllable, and so is the *kyl* (but the *a* in *alone* is a syllable by itself). Readers often recognize familiar syllables in familiar locations and use them in decoding. Notice the familiar location and pronunciation of the rime -*ine* in *fine, kine, dine, line, mine, nine, pine, vine, spine*, and so on. Or the -*one* in *alone, bone, cone, drone, hone, phone, stone, tone*, and *zone* (notice too that the familiar words *done, gone*, and *none* deviate from the pattern). Changing the location of the -*ine* changes its syllable pattern and signaled pronunciation, as in *inert, inept*, and *inexact*. Not all patterns are equally stable, but in certain predictable locations syllable patterns are often quite stable and useful in decoding.

Words are also structured into meaning units called *morphemes*. Like syllables, every word has at least one morpheme but may have more. However, morphemes do not correspond exactly with syllables. The roots, prefixes, and suffixes of words are common morphemes. Compound words are simply words with two roots, as in *gentleman*. Addition of the adverb-producing suffix -*ly* makes the word *gentlemanly*, and addition of the negative prefix *un*- makes the word *ungentlemanly*, a total of four morphemes (but five syllables). Other morphemes may not be as easy to distinguish depending on familiarity. *Alkyl* is a familiar morpheme in chemistry, signifying a hydrocarbon. Also familiar to a chemist are *benzyl, methyl*, and *ammonium*. The word *alkylbenzyldimethylammonium* may be decoded in different chunks by different readers depending on their prior knowledge. Chemists would be likely to perceive morphemes, while others may deal more with syllables, or even individual graphemes and phonemes in places.

Decoding works optimally when morphemes are taken onto account. For example, the vowel combination *oi* is often associated with the phoneme /oy/, as in the words *oil*, *coin*, *point*, and *avoid*. However, notice the pronunciation difference for *oi* in *boing*, *going*, *doing*, or *booing*. In the last three words the -*ing* forms a suffix added to the roots *go*, *do*, and *boo*, breaking up the pronunciation of *oi*. Likewise, *th* is a digraph (a phonic unit with two letters representing one sound) in *another* and *toothache*, but not in *sweetheart* or *masthead*; *ph* is a digraph in *telephone* and *alphabet*, but not in *shepherd* or *haphazard*; *sh* is a digraph in *wishes* and *fashion*, but not in *mishap* or *dishonest*. Divisions between morphemes govern pronunciation as well as syllable divisions and phonics generalizations.

Sight Vocabulary

Another way words are decoded is "automatically" as wholes, without the analysis and synthesis involved in phonics and structural analysis. Some words don't easily lend themselves to analysis. Many everyday words deviate at least in part from common phonics patterns—for example, *done*, *gone*, *none*, *the*, *of*, *are*, *have*, *come*, *were*, *what*, *been*, *know*, and *there*. Such words become so familiar that they are recognized instantly, like old friends. When we read our own name we don't sound it out by letter or syllable even though the spelling may be uncommon. We even learn common phrases this way, such as *rock 'n' roll*, *hip-hop*, *hot dog*, *air-conditioned*, and so on. As we grow in reading ability, more and more words become sight words, so that only new words require extensive, conscious analysis. A chemist might even recognize *alkylbenzyldimethylammonium* by sight if he or she encountered it with sufficient regularity! Developing an extensive sight vocabulary is a major aspect of fluent reading.

As we saw in Chapter 2, a traditional method of teaching beginning reading is to teach a sight vocabulary of 50 words or so that is learned by repetition (e.g., via repetitive sentences, flash cards) and then to teach simple phonic generalizations using analytic phonics or reasoning by analogy. An example of reasoning by analogy is learning the words *dish*, *win*, and *fell*, and then removing the initial consonants *d*, *w*, and *f* and cross-combining them with the remaining parts to form *wish*, *well*, *fin*, *dell*, *fish*, and *din*. Another sight vocabulary method involves teaching of a select list of words of such high frequency that they make up the bulk of printed English (*the*, *of*, *and*, *a*, *to*, *in*, *is*, *you*, *that*, *it*, etc.). Research estimates suggest that about 100 words make up 50% of all written English! Of course, sight word learning, phonics, and structural analysis are often combined in various ways in teaching decoding.

Context

Context in decoding involves the use of our intuitive knowledge of grammar and meaning. Grammatical cues are signaled within a sentence and may involve little meaning. For example, consider the pseudoword *bipled* (Sadoski & Paivio, 2001). It has no known meaning, but several pronunciations are likely including *bi pled*, *bi pld*, and *bip ld*. Which pronunciation applies is partly a matter of grammar as signaled by the word's syntax, or position in a sentence. For example, consider the sentence *The glork bipled the slink.* Here, the pseudoword *bipled* is in a verb position, the *-ed* is interpreted as a past tense verb suffix, and the pronunciations *bip ld* and *bi pld* are more probable. But in the sentence *A slink is a bipled*, the pseudoword *bipled* is in a noun position and the *bi-* might be interpreted as a prefix meaning "two," perhaps by association with the word *biped*. Because of the lack of a known meaning we can't be sure, but context reduces possibilities and provides hints. In the sentence *Oswiecim is the Polish name for Auschwitz* the grammatical class and meaning of *Oswiecim* are both clear, even if the pronunciation isn't. For centuries, many beginning reading books have also provided pictures that give hints and form a part of the context in addition to the print.

Context often serves to limit what a word might be, but in some cases it actually determines what a word is. One category of words is *heteronyms*, single spellings with different meanings and pronunciations. These are words like *bass*, *tear*, *lead*, *bow*, *wind*, *wound*, *console*, *dove*, *minute*, and *project*. Context here determines which meaning and consequent pronunciation applies to these common words (*bass* drum, largemouth *bass*; *minute* hand, *minute* detail; etc.). That is, context alone determines word identification in these cases.

Context serves a kind of reciprocal relationship with phonics, structural analysis, and sight words. Knowing what a word is likely to be from the words around it assists in decoding, but a reader must have already decoded some of the words for there to be a context, and round and round it goes. We might imagine a reader as a juggler who has to keep a few different objects in the air at once. Individual differences in ability and instruction may affect whether phonics, structural analysis, sight vocabulary, or context strategies are most preferred by different readers, but readers rely on them all to some extent. Juggling only one won't do the trick. This is what decoding is really all about in practice.

Dictionary

Dictionaries provide all the information necessary for proper decoding: pronunciations, grammatical classes, meanings, morphemes, common variations, and so on. Of course, a general degree of reading ability and some specialized skills are needed for effective dictionary use, but dictionaries and glossaries at different reading levels are widely available and a variety, including picture dictionaries, are usually found in schools.

Dictionaries have limitations, as do all the other decoding methods. Some definitions have been known to be circular (e.g., concept—idea; idea—concept), and some verbose (vector—a directed line segment representing both magnitude and direction such as force or velocity). Some of this is unavoidable due to the re-flexive quality of language (i.e., using language to define language), but dictionaries continue to improve since the first ones appeared less than 400 years ago (Shakespeare had none!).

Few reference books are as useful as a dictionary for developing an independent ability to read and a rich vocabulary. But because consulting a dictionary causes a disruption in reading, we often avoid its use or put it off until a more opportune moment, relying on the adage "When all else fails, look it up." Many readers are probably underskilled and undermotivated in the use of this reference tool.

COMPREHENSION

If decoding is *saying* something, comprehension is *understanding* something, getting its meaning. This is the second fundamental competency of reading, and the central one. Whereas decoding in-volves producing a spoken analog of printed language, comprehen-sion involves producing a thought analog of printed language. This is decoding in the general sense rather than in the special sense peculiar to reading. In this sense, comprehension is the reconstruction of the author's message—the author constructs a message and encodes it in printed language, and the reader decodes the printed language and reconstructs the message. When all goes well, communication oc-curs—two minds with one thought and the implications of that thought.

In the sense of communication, the word *understanding* can be taken literally; we "stand under" the author's message, subordinat-ing our own interpretations to try to grasp the author's intentions, even when we suspect the author is trying to deceive us. However, reading need not stop with understanding. Reading at its fullest in-cludes reflecting on what is read, evaluating it, comparing it with what is already known from other reading or from direct experi-ence, trying it on for size to see how it fits.

The previous section showed how using context is one aspect of decoding. Context implicates grammar and morphology in decoding, and therefore meaning to some degree. However, there are aspects of comprehension that go far beyond using context to decode words. Probably the simplest and best way to understand this is to view comprehension as occurring in levels. Three levels of comprehension are usually proposed: the *literal* level, the *inferential* or *interpretive* level, and the *critical, applied,* or *appreciative* level. William S. Gray (1960) lucidly called the three levels *reading the lines, reading between the lines,* and *reading beyond the lines.* We will deal with the first two levels here; the third level is dealt with in the following section on response.

The Literal Level

This level involves literal comprehension, interpreting the author's words in a given sentence in a way that has meaning to us, but without considering and weighing the implications of any interpretation we may have. Literal comprehension involves word meaning, but it is more than decoding the meanings of individual words one at a time. Context determines word meaning to a great extent.

Consider the three words *the, ship,* and *sinks.* Two very different sentences can be composed from these words. *The ship sinks* could mean a large boat descending below the water. But *Ship the sinks* means to transport kitchen or bathroom appliances. The difference in word order, or syntax, causes the words to mean different things. Few words have only one meaning, and context determines which meaning applies. Literal comprehension does not deal with our interpretations of why the ship might have sunk, how big the ship was, or whether it sank in freshwater or at sea. Literal comprehension does not deal with whether the sinks were kitchen or bathroom sinks, or both, or where the sinks were being shipped to or from, or much else. We may have such interpretations, but they cannot be verified from the words of the text; they are not literal ("of the letters").

Literal comprehension deals only with the textually explicit, with what is directly stated. This is important in legal documents, for example. Consider the hypothetical case of the will of a rich uncle leaving $1 million each to "Mary, Jim, Sue and John." If Sue and John are a couple, there is ambiguity about whether Sue and John get $1 million each or whether Sue and John get $1 million together as a couple. But a comma after Sue means $1 million each. Literal language can be important!

Comprehension questions at the literal level have answers that are stated explicitly, "right there." In the sentence *The kids crept toward the old, deserted house* we might ask who crept toward the old, deserted house. The answer (the kids) is literally stated, and therefore the question taps the literal level of comprehension. However, to press the point a bit, what exactly is meant by *kids*? This word can mean children, but also young goats. Conceivably, some young goats might be creeping toward the old, deserted house. This interpretation is unlikely because of the communicative aspect of comprehension: part of the implied contract between authors and readers is that ordinary, default assumptions apply unless the author signals differently. The answer to this question might be clearly resolved in the next sentence, but there is nothing literal in this sentence to prevent the goat interpretation, however unlikely. The point is that the concept of literal comprehension is a very restricted, verbal one. It mainly answers the question "What does this say, exactly?"

The Inferential or Interpretive Level

The level of inferential comprehension, also called the interpretive level, is the level of comprehending what is implied but not explicitly stated. The morphemes that make up *infer* mean "to carry into," implying that we carry meaning into a text rather than draw it out. There is probably no comprehension without some degree of inference (Were those "kids" children or goats?). As we have shown, inference produced by context is helpful and sometimes necessary in decoding to speech and determining literal meaning, so the boundary between decoding and comprehension is a bit blurry—to a degree, we are always reading between the lines. But inferential, interpretive comprehension goes far beyond the determination of word meanings. It is involved with building a mental model of the whole situation implied by the text with reasonable certainty. What we mean by a "mental model" is a coherent image of a situation, either actual or fictional, that is consistent with the language of the text (Sadoski & Paivio, 2001).

Inferences can be broadly classified as logical or pragmatic. *Logical inferences* involve the rules of formal logic and result in a high degree of certainty. If A = B and B = C, then A = C by simple verbal syllogism. If Jim is taller than Mary, and Mary is taller than Sue, then Jim is taller than Sue. The mental model here might involve imagining the characters lined up by height. However, consider two other situations. If Jim is taller than Mary, and Sue is taller than Mary, Mary is the shortest but we cannot logically determine who is the tallest. The sentence *Jim isn't as tall as Mary, but Mary is shorter than Jim* is logically inconsistent, and cannot be imagined in any real or fictional world. It doesn't "make sense."

Pragmatic inferences are situation-specific and generally occur with a lower degree of certainty. Consider these two sentences together: *The kids crept toward the old, deserted house. The flashlight beam trembled.* Notice how your mind immediately pulls them together into a little episode and invests the episode with unstated information. In a complete mental model, we might supply a time, a setting, characters with ages and genders, and even their emotional state. Notice the reasoning involved in answering the following two inferential questions:

- What time of day is it? (Probably night because the flashlight was on and it's creepier to sneak up on old, deserted houses at night.)

- What mood were the kids in? (Probably afraid; the flashlight beam was in a hand trembling with fear).

Notice also our continued use of the word *probably*. Because they are implicit rather than explicit, pragmatic inferences exist with a degree of probability less than certainty. When formal logic is involved, the probability becomes certainty as long as the premises are true. The answers to the inferential questions just given are highly probable, but not completely certain. The hour could be daylight and the trembling hand could be due to infirmity. (The "kids" could even be goats in a fantasy tale like those of Dr. Seuss or C. S. Lewis.) Other inferences such as the location of the house or the number, ages, and genders of the kids would have still less probability and might vary considerably between readers.

Such inferences are often made on the basis of information beyond the sentence. Where such information is unavailable, such as at the very beginning of a story, inferences are made provisionally. As noted earlier, authors are obliged to provide critical information, but no author is ever completely explicit about every detail of time, place, character, and so on. Much is left unsaid for the reader to fill in. If literal comprehension generally answers the question "What does this say?", inferential comprehension generally answers the question "What does this mean?"

RESPONSE

When we ask if someone has read Plato we aren't asking if that person has decoded Plato accurately, or even if that person has understood all the particulars of Plato's intended meanings. We are mainly asking what that person thinks of having read Plato, how he or she interprets it. The third fundamental competency of reading involves a personal reaction to what is read, the contemplation of the ideas and feelings evoked by the text, responding to the text both cognitively and affectively. Some prefer to think that this is no longer a part of the reading process, but a reflection on what has been read. Others prefer to think of this as the third level of comprehension that completes the reading act. In either case, this competency involves reading beyond the lines, going beyond literal statement and inferential probability to finding personal relevance and significance. Here the reader answers the question "What does this mean to me?"

This level of reading has been alternatively called the *critical* level, the *applied* level, and the *appreciative* level, among other labels. While these terms are not exactly synonymous, they are all common, overlapping varieties of response.

Critical Reading

Critical reading involves assessing and judging the value of what is read. Reading critically can be seen as a conversation with an author, talking back to an author in our imagination. Adler and Van Doren, in their classic *How to Read a Book* (1972, pp. 137–139) summarized it like this:

> Reading a book is a kind of conversation. You may think it is not a conversation at all, because the author does all the talking and you have nothing to say. If you think that, you do not recognize your full obligation as a reader—and you are not grasping your opportunities. . . . A good book deserves an active reading. The activity of reading does not stop with the work of understanding what a book says. *It must be completed by the work of criticism, the work of judging.*

Critical reading means evaluating and judging, but a good critic does more than retort with thumbs-up, thumbs-down verdicts. A good critic engages in the task of looking deeper and appraising relative strengths and weaknesses. Critical reading involves an open-minded assessment of a work's form, style, credibility, depth, and relative stature among other works of the same kind. It involves gaining insight and enlightenment as well as detecting bias and propaganda. As Sir Francis Bacon once warned, we should not read to contradict and confute, nor to believe and take for granted, but to weigh and consider. In the last chapter we presented Goal 2: Developing Personal Interests and Tastes in Reading. Critical reading involves developing discriminating tastes based on standards of value, either public or private.

Application

Application involves the construction of knowledge by the reader, particularly for the purpose of carrying that knowledge beyond the text. This amounts to learning, where *learning* is traditionally defined as a potential or actual change in behavior as a result of instruction or experience. Chapter 3 noted the transition between learning to read and reading to learn. Reading to learn is a central part of much schooling, where what we learn through reading is put to work both in and out of school.

Learning through reading involves the connection between what the reader already knows and what he or she encounters anew in the text, a fusion of the two that causes growth and change in the reader. Such changes are not necessarily large, dramatic, or sudden; learning through reading is often cumulative and slow, although flashes of insight do occur from time to time. Examples of learning through reading for application were seen in the last chapter under Goal 3: Developing the Use of Reading as a Tool to Solve Problems. Such problems can be personal or social, including academic problems, and of small or large scale.

School-related problems (reading to learn) and work-related problems (reading to do) were discussed in Chapter 3. A key school-related example of application learning is acquiring study skills such as locating, organizing, and retaining information from text for projects, reports, or tests. A key work-related example involves professionals in any field reading professional literature and applying new principles, practices, or products in the office, school,

73

hospital, business, and so on. On the personal side, self-help litera-ture is widely available for application to personal issues.

Appreciation

Reader response can take the form of "living through" a text. This can be seen as a major aspect of literary appreciation, where a reader constructs a mental model or inner world where the settings, characters, and events come alive far beyond what the author may have described or implied and what the reader might have ever be-fore imagined. The reader may have a favorite fictional work where the characters and settings reside in memory with as much reality as actual persons or places. The immense popularity of the Harry Potter books or *The Lord of the Rings* trilogy by J. R. R. Tolkein serve as current cultural examples.

Appreciation also can be seen as an extension of critical read-ing, where through careful evaluation and discrimination readers personalize the challenging new ideas or experiences they encoun-ter and develop heightened internal standards. This was briefly discussed in the last chapter under Goal 2: Developing Personal In-terests and Tastes in Reading. However, literary experiences do not enjoy a monopoly on appreciation. Readers can gain expansive and profound experiences from nonfiction where biography, history, or even science and mathematics come to life with personal relevance or their ability to crystallize ideas with elegance.

Not all reading requires the same level of response. Everyday, mundane reading tasks call for little, whereas serious text encoun-ters require more. But even in everyday tasks, response is more a part of reading than we might assume. Even as we sort through the day's mail, we make continuous judgments about what to discard, what can wait till later, and what to read with close attention imme-diately. A sign reading *Please Keep Off the Grass* elicits different responses from casual pedestrians or firefighters approaching a burning building. Following a recipe may seem like a clear case of direct application, but probably few recipes are followed to the letter without some personal variations by expert chefs or even daring novices. In any case, no full account of reading can omit response, and no reading curriculum would be complete without attention to it.

THE FIRST CONTINUUM: PRINT INPUT
VERSUS READER INPUT

The three fundamental competencies of reading discussed in this chapter can be arrayed on an underlying continuum that unifies them. We call this "the first continuum" because the next chapter presents a second continuum dealing with teaching and learning. These two continua together form the overall conceptual framework for teaching reading presented in this book.

Reading has two sources in this continuum. One source is something to be read, generally referred to as the print, and the other source is the reader. Reading cannot occur without input from both sources. Although input from either the print or the reader can be increased or decreased to a degree, neither can ever be increased to 100% or reduced to 0%—some of each is always required in reading. An unopened book is not being read, and a mind not engaged by text is not reading. Depending on the relative amount of input from one source or the other, reading can be conceptualized as one of the three fundamental competencies. The continuum between input from the print and input from the reader with the three fundamental competencies arrayed is shown in Figure 4.1.

When input from the print is primary and input from the reader is secondary, reading becomes most like decoding. The print takes prominence here because that is where the message is encoded; it is a portal through which we must pass. Alphabetic print maps the speech of its respective language, and so some degree of speech recoding is involved in reading even if subconsciously. However, it would be too easy to conclude that this com-

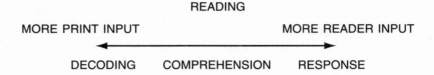

FIGURE 4.1. The three fundamental competencies of reading and their underlying continuum between *more print input* and *more reader input*.

petency of reading was the primary competency to be learned before the other competencies apply. That is, it is tempting to think of reading as recoding printed language to spoken language and then simply listening to yourself talk. Unfortunately, decoding overlaps with comprehension (as explained earlier) and the boundary between the two is not as distinct as is sometimes assumed.

Comprehension is central to reading. It occupies the central place on the continuum where input from the print and input from the reader are in relative balance. The print is important here in gaining the particulars of the message, but the reader's inferential interpretation of the print is equally important. However carefully an author composes a text, a reader must fill in what was necessarily left unsaid in order to comprehend. In doing so, the reader's mind contributes to the reading as much or more than the print does. At some point, the boundary between comprehension and response is crossed, so this boundary is indistinct as well.

Response occurs toward the end of the continuum where input from the reader becomes more important than input from the print, where the print serves merely as a springboard for our own mental critique, application, or appreciation. As noted earlier, this may be seen as responding to something already read, and surely response can occur long after the printed text has been put aside. But responding to our meanings is an aspect of reading both conceptually and educationally. In the next two chapters we turn to education and teaching issues more directly.

REFERENCES

Adler, M., & Van Doren, C. (1972). *How to read a book* (rev. ed.). New York: Simon & Schuster.

Daniels, L. B. (1970). The concept of reading. Part I: Reading as saying. *Journal of Education, 16,* 1–26.

Daniels, L. B. (1980). The concept of reading. Part II: Reading as comprehending. In *Philosophy of education: 1979* (pp. 151–161). Normal: Philosophy of Education Society, Illinois State University.

Daniels, L. B. (1982). The concept of reading: Reading as thinking. In *Philosophy of education: 1981* (pp. 309–317). Normal: Philosophy of Education Society, Illinois State University.

Gray, W. S. (1960). The major aspects of reading. In H. M. Robinson (Ed.), *Sequential development of reading abilities* (supplementary educational monographs, no. 90, pp. 8–24). Chicago: University of Chicago Press.

Ryle, G. (1949). *The concept of mind.* New York: Barnes and Noble.

Sadoski, M. (1982). *A study of the theoretical bases of reading instruction and a comparison of programs.* Texas A&M University Instructional Research Laboratory Technical Paper No. R83001. (ERIC Document Reproduction Service No. ED 236 543)

Sadoski, M., & Paivio, A. (2001). *Imagery and text: A dual coding theory of reading and writing.* Mahwah, NJ: Erlbaum.

CHAPTER 5

How?

Part I. Basic Teaching
and Learning Approaches

The teaching and learning of reading can be conceptualized as many variations on a few themes. Our discussion of the teaching and learning of reading is divided into three parts. Part I, covered in this chapter, defines three themes or basic teaching and learning approaches and locates them on an underlying continuum. Part II, discussed in Chapter 6, combines those three basic teaching and learning approaches with the three fundamental competencies of reading that were discussed earlier in Chapter 4. Together they form the conceptual framework for teaching reading presented in this book. Part III, presented in Chapter 7, elaborates on the concept of a balanced approach to teaching reading through some key principles and practices.

THE SECOND CONTINUUM:
INSTRUCTION VERSUS EDUCATION

All teaching and learning in reading can be arrayed on an underlying continuum between the two poles *instruction* and *education* (shown in Figure 5.1). These two terms are here used as polar opposites although they are often used as synonyms in general discussions. Explicitly defining these terms will clarify this opposition.

The word *instruct* comes from the two Latin morphemes *in*, meaning in, and *structus*, meaning to build or arrange (hence the word *structure*). To *instruct*, therefore, literally means to place a structure into something, to build into. When we instruct learners, we have a structure of knowledge outside of the learners that we build into them. *Instruction*, then, means to put a structure of knowledge in from without. The teacher has it, the learners do not, and the teacher builds it into them.

This form of teaching has a long and proud history from time immemorial when someone who knew something explained it to someone else, or someone who knew how to do something showed someone else how to do it. This is teaching as telling, showing, demonstrating, and arranging a course of lessons to be completed as steps in acquiring the information or the skill. This approach places the learners in a relatively subordinate role, subject to the direction of the teacher and the course of lessons, although the learners must ultimately internalize the learning for themselves.

Conversely, the word *educate* comes from the two Latin morphemes *e*, meaning out, and *ductus*, meaning to lead or draw (hence the word *duct*). To *educate*, therefore, literally means to lead

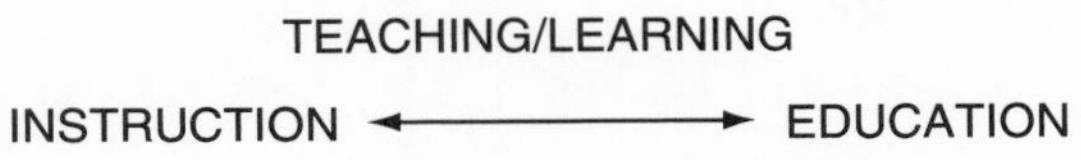

TEACHING/LEARNING

INSTRUCTION ◄──────► EDUCATION

FIGURE 5.1. The underlying continuum of teaching/learning between *instruction* and *education*.

or draw out. When we educate learners, we draw the desired knowledge or skill out of them. *Education*, then, means to draw learning out from within. In this sense, it is the polar opposite of putting learning in from without.

This form of teaching and learning also has a proud history dating back to antiquity. One of its earliest demonstrations is found in Plato's *Meno* where Socrates helps an uneducated slave child to realize a geometric theorem without giving him any instruction in geometry. The slave's realization comes about via Socrates' use of careful questions that eliminate what could not be true and then develop what is true (hence the Socratic method). Socrates' point was that all learning exists in potential form within the learner, to be realized by careful extraction. The role of the teacher in this instance is to prompt, guide, and monitor as the learners work to form knowledge and skill from within. This approach places learners in a relatively more dominant role because internal control and motivation are more central, although they are still under the direction of a teacher.

All teaching and learning can be seen as occurring somewhere between the two poles of instruction and education. While the extremes are perhaps seldom practiced, it is difficult to overstate how basic this continuum is in the teaching profession, its history, and its debates. The educational philosopher John Dewey in his book *Experience and Education* (1938, p. 17) summarized it this way:

> The history of educational theory is marked by the opposition between the idea that education is developed from within and that it is formation from without; that it is based upon natural endowments and that education is a process of overcoming natural inclination and substituting in its place habits acquired under external pressure.

Forming from without or developing from within are the two extremes of the continuum, and three basic teaching/learning approaches in reading can be arrayed along this continuum.

THE THREE BASIC TEACHING/LEARNING
APPROACHES IN READING

Chapter 4 explained how reading always involves two parties: the printed text and the reader. Whenever the teaching of reading occurs, a third party is added to the scene: the teacher. Depending on which party is dominant and which parties are subordinate, three possible triads, three basic teaching/learning approaches, can occur. Most of the rest of this chapter discusses each of these triads in turn.

In the following discussions, the definition of the printed text will necessarily be expanded. In the modern history of teaching reading, the single printed text has given way to a full program of text materials, complete with various books, teachers' manuals, workbooks, kits, games, software, tests, and other supplementary materials. In many cases, the elements of these programs are carefully coordinated and sequenced. More or less of such material is inherent in different methods, and more or less of such material may be used in different situations, depending on curriculum constraints, the inclination and training of teachers, available instructional time, funding, and so on. The point is that the printed text materials that are used in the teaching of reading are typically extensive and systematically organized into programs. These programs can become the dominant member of the triad.

Program-Controlled Teaching/Learning

In program-controlled teaching/learning, the program is dominant and the teacher and the reader are subordinate. Figure 5.2 illustrates this arrangement.

Notice the line extending from this triad to the end of the continuum labeled *instruction*. When programs control the teaching/learning situation, the structure of lessons and activities is planned externally and delivered through the teacher to the readers. The teacher and readers work together in following the lessons and ac-

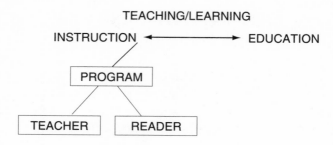

FIGURE 5.2. Program-controlled teaching/learning and its location on the continuum.

tivities as planned. Hence, the structure of knowledge and skill is imposed from without, and this arrangement is therefore more associated with the instructional end of the continuum.

Many reading programs are commercially produced by publishing companies and marketed to schools. Basal reader programs or skills management programs are examples. Experts are employed by the publishers to plan the sequence of lessons and activities and produce the corresponding materials. An appropriate scope of learnings is determined for each grade level, and lessons are carefully designed and sequenced to reinforce existing learnings and introduce new ones on a schedule. These lessons are delivered through the materials provided, typically one or more books per student for each grade level with various supplements, as described before.

This approach is associated with dividing reading into a set of skills to be separately taught and then assembled into the complete reading act. This is done in accordance with the three fundamental competencies described in Chapter 4: decoding, comprehension, and response. Decoding is divided into a set of skills including phonics skills, structural analysis skills, sight vocabulary skills, context skills, and dictionary or reference skills. Comprehension is divided into literal comprehension skills, inferential or interpretive comprehension skills, and critical, applied, or appreciative comprehension skills. Response is usually treated as the final level of comprehension.

Each of these sets of skills can be further divided into subskills. For example, decoding can be subdivided into learning consonant and vowel sounds and phonic generalizations for their combinations, learning common morphemes and syllable divisions, learning high-frequency words by sight, learning to use various kinds of context clues, and so on. Comprehension can be subdivided into explicitly locating or inferring main ideas and details, causes and effects, comparisons and contrasts, sequences of events in a narrative or points in an exposition, predicting outcomes, discriminating fact from opinion, judging the actions of characters, and so on. The extent of the subdivision of skills differs between programs. Some have only a few subdivisions—others have a great many subdivisions, up to hundreds in some cases.

This approach has great appeal for systematic, organized teaching and testing. In programs called "skills management programs" a systematic procedure of test–teach–retest is followed for each subskill. This allows for considerable individualization of progress: some learners move ahead quickly while other learners redo skills units (usually an alternate unit on the same content) until a test criterion is reached. The extensive record keeping entailed is accomplished with the help of computers in some programs. Instruction in such cases is heavily clerical and technological whether computers are used or not. This has led to the criticism that such teaching is remote and mechanical, but this need not be the case where teachers have humane concern for their students' individual differences and problems.

A key part of the delivery of a basal reader program is the teacher's guide, one or more manuals with explicit directions or suggestions to the teacher for delivering the program materials. For each individual lesson, the teacher's guide will generally include prereading activities (e.g., new vocabulary to be introduced), during-reading activities (e.g., a purpose for reading to be assigned), and postreading activities (e.g., comprehension questions and model answers). Some teacher's guides provide actual scripts for the teacher to follow. Extensive directions for supplementary follow-up activities and their materials are included in the teacher's guide as well. If teachers follow these instructions with little deviation, the program rather than the teacher controls the teaching/learning. In their most extreme form, reading instruction programs can all but remove the teacher from the triad. However, most teachers use professional judgment in modifying such programs to fit differing situations.

Teacher-Controlled Teaching/Learning

In teacher-controlled teaching/learning, the teacher is dominant and the program and the readers are subordinate. In this approach, the teachers determine the learning conditions according to their professional training, experience, and judgment. Programs and text materials are used according to those determinations, and readers are subject to those determinations. Figure 5.3 illustrates this arrangement.

Notice that this triad is found at the center of the continuum, with lines extending toward both the *instruction* end of the continuum and the *education* end of the continuum. This implies that the teacher has wide latitude concerning how teaching is carried out. In

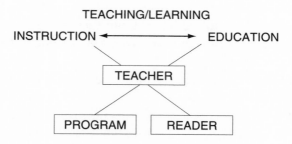

FIGURE 5.3. Teacher-controlled teaching/learning and its location on the continuum.

effect, the teacher is in a pivotal position where one of the two extremes is approximated or where some intermediate approach is used.

If the teacher decides to deliver one or more selected programs, or coordinated parts of selected programs, using the specific directions supplied, his or her teaching most resembles instruction. In fact, if the teacher were to use one program completely according to its directions, the situation would amount to program-controlled teaching/learning, consistent with the continuum. If the teacher works cooperatively with readers in teaching according to their needs or interests, using methods and materials that are largely student-centered, the situation more resembles education. This arrangement is discussed in the next section.

However, the primary characteristic of this approach is the teacher as decision maker. The teacher may decide to be a purveyor of programs or to serve as a facilitator of student-centered learning, but teachers are more likely to selectively combine different methods and materials in their own individual ways. A nearly limitless variety of combinations of methods and materials is possible. We mention several common combinations here; in the next chapter we discuss others.

Over many years, research on the use of reading methods and materials has consistently indicated that reading teachers often use a modified basal reader approach (Cloud-Silva & Sadoski, 1987; McKenna, Kear, & Ellsworth, 1995). This combination involves the selective use of basal reader lessons, supplemented with additional teacher-prepared lessons to emphasize areas of need as determined by the teacher. Supplementary lessons typically involve additional instruction in decoding or reading authentic literature. In this combination, the teacher does not use the basal every day, but selects basal lessons for use on some days. On other days, the teacher may instruct students in phonics, structural analysis, context clues, and so on. On still other days, the students may read self-selected books in order to build fluency, increase their appreciation, pursue interests, solve problems, and integrate reading skills. Different combinations are often used for subgroups of students with different needs, interests, or abilities. Such combinations traditionally lean toward the instruction end of the continuum, although they contain elements of both ends.

In some cases, teachers may invent methods and materials of their own. This may include selecting or even writing texts across content areas and inventing projects to ensure the comprehension of those texts. In some historical cases, necessity has been the mother of invention. The language experience approach (Chapter 2), in which students' own oral speech is transcribed and used as material for teaching them to read, was used in remote areas where books were unavailable. We will return to this method soon. The latitude for invention and discovery in the teaching of reading is a great avenue for teacher creativity.

Reader-Controlled Teaching/Learning

In reader-controlled teaching/learning, the reader is dominant and the teacher and the program are subordinate. Figure 5.4 illustrates this arrangement.

Notice the line extending from this triad to the end of the continuum labeled *education*. When the teaching/learning situation is reader-centered, the internal motivation and ability of the readers

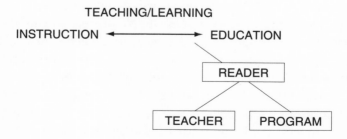

FIGURE 5.4. Reader-controlled teaching/learning and its location on the continuum.

take the lead, and teachers and text programs are used as resources for the readers' learning requirements. This does not mean that teacher guidance and authority are eliminated, only that readers provide the primary direction for their own learning. Hence, knowledge and skill are developed more from within, and the arrangement is more associated with the education end of the continuum.

Rather than a subskills approach with a scope and sequence of external introduction and reinforcement, this approach involves students developing the fundamental competencies as they use them. Rather than adapting readers to the material, the material is adapted to the readers. Reading materials often come from various content areas and the curriculum becomes more integrated rather than separated into reading lessons, mathematics lessons, science lessons, and so on. This approach is typically more holistic than the subskills approach.

An example of a student-centered approach to beginning reading is the language experience approach. In this approach students share a common experience, say, a holiday or field trip. The reading lesson involves each student in a small group orally composing a sentence about the experience. Each sentence is written down by the teacher on a large chart for all to see. The teacher then reads the sentence back, pointing to the words, and the student checks for accuracy. The student and the teacher next read the sentence orally together, perhaps several times, and the student eventually attempts to orally read it alone with teacher help as needed. Over several lessons, the sentences of each member of the group are learned by all, and a brief text can then be read independently.

This text is then used for additional reading instruction. High-frequency words used in different sentences (e.g., *and, the, is, are*) are identified for sight learning. Other words can be compared for phonic similarities. Common morphemes can be learned (e.g., the plural suffixes *-s* or *-es*). Known words can be rearranged into new sentences to employ grammar and context. In short, the students have produced their own text and reading lessons with teacher guidance and assistance. The original experience may involve content from nearly any familiar field, cutting across curriculum divisions.

Examples of this teaching/learning approach for more advanced students include individualized reading, where students self-select books with teacher guidance based on interest, ability, and other factors. Students then confer regularly with the teacher to answer questions, clarify misunderstandings, summarize, read orally to check decoding progress, and so on.

Reader-centered teaching/learning is often highly individualized and does not afford the technical convenience of record keeping offered by program-controlled approaches. The integration of the curriculum rather than the separate teaching of separate subjects poses further organizational concerns for some. Despite such challenges, this approach is a viable one that is at least partially practiced in many classrooms.

Figure 5.5 presents the three fundamental teaching/learning approaches on their underlying continuum. As implied by the continuum, many combinations and variations of these three themes are composed and orchestrated by teachers. Some have been dis-

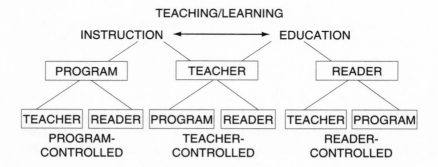

FIGURE 5.5. The three fundamental teaching/learning approaches on their underlying continuum.

cussed in this chapter and more are discussed in the next chapter. This general conceptual framework can account for virtually all the practices in the teaching of reading that have been developed throughout its history.

REACHING DIFFERENT GOALS
WITH DIFFERENT APPROACHES

Research on the learning outcomes of different teaching/learning approaches has revealed an interesting and important trend: different approaches tend to produce different results in different domains of learning. Recall that Chapter 3 defined the domains of learning and presented four goals of teaching reading, two in the affective domain and two in the cognitive domain. Researchers have compared the different teaching/learning approaches defined in this chapter on how successfully they serve to reach those goals.

Research synthesis is the field of research that combines the findings of many individual studies in a given area. Over many decades, numerous individual studies have been conducted on the learning outcomes characteristic of different teaching/learning approaches. In several large-scale studies combining huge bodies of evidence, Walberg and others synthesized this data into general conclusions about the outcomes of several different teaching/learning approaches corresponding to those defined here (e.g., Walberg, 1986; Walberg & Waxman, 1983; Wang, Haertel, & Walberg, 1993).

As defined here, program-controlled teaching/learning is most related to the *instruction* end of the continuum, reader-controlled teaching/learning is most related to the *education* end of the continuum, and teacher-controlled teaching/learning varies between the two continua, but is traditionally closer to the *instruction* end. A key conclusion of the research synthesis is that teaching/learning approaches that emphasize instruction tend to be somewhat more successful at producing cognitive outcomes but somewhat less successful at producing affective outcomes. Conversely, teaching/ learning approaches that emphasize education tend to be somewhat more successful at producing affective outcomes but somewhat less successful at producing cognitive outcomes.

While the differences were not great, Walberg (1986) concluded that students in classes that emphasized education over instruction did slightly to no worse on standardized achievement tests, including reading tests, and slightly to substantially better on outcomes such as positive attitudes, curiosity, cooperativeness, and independence—outcomes more affective in nature. Unless the approach was extreme, approaches more directed toward education enhanced affective results without detracting from cognitive results. Where the approaches were extreme, there was an increasing trade-off between cognitive outcomes and affective outcomes. Chapter 8 explains that little difference has been found in either student achievement or student attitude between these two broad approaches when applied to teaching reading, but attitude is only one aspect of the affective domain.

What this suggests to the reading teacher is that some combination of instruction and education may be best for reaching all the goals presented in Chapter 3. Teachers might be best advised to find a balanced approach most suitable for each situation to realize all the goals. More discussion of these goals in the specific context of reading methods is discussed in the next chapter.

REFERENCES

Cloud-Silva, C., & Sadoski, M. (1987). Reading teachers' attitudes toward basal reader use and state adoption policies. *Journal of Educational Research, 81*, 5–16.

Dewey, J. (1938). *Experience and education*. New York: Collier Books.

McKenna, M. C., Kear, D. J., & Ellsworth, R. A. (1995). Children's attitudes toward reading: A national survey. *Reading Research Quarterly, 30*, 934–956.

Walberg, H. J. (1986). Synthesis of research on teaching. In M. C. Wittrock (Ed.), *Handbook of research on teaching* (3rd ed., pp. 214–229). New York: Macmillan.

Walberg, H. J., & Waxman, H. C. (1983). Teaching, learning, and the management of instruction. In D. C. Smith (Ed.), *Essential knowledge for beginning educators* (pp. 38–54). Washington, DC: American Association of Colleges for Teacher Education and ERIC Clearinghouse on Teacher Education.

Wang, M. C., Haertel, G. D., & Walberg, H. J. (1993). Toward a knowledge base for school learning. *Review of Educational Research, 63,* 249–294.

CHAPTER 6

How?

Part II. A Map of the Territory

The previous two chapters presented two continua, one for the three fundamental competencies of reading (Chapter 4), and the other for three fundamental teaching/learning approaches used in teaching reading (Chapter 5). The three fundamental competencies of reading on the first continuum were decoding, comprehension, and response. This is what we teach readers to do. The three fundamental teaching/learning approaches on the second continuum were program-controlled teaching/learning, teacher-controlled teaching/learning, and reader-controlled teaching/learning. These are the ways in which we teach readers to do it. This chapter coordinates these two dimensions into an overall map of the territory of teaching reading and then locates some well-known approaches and methods on this map.

Logically, if we coordinate the three fundamental competencies with the three fundamental teaching/learning approaches, we have nine different combinations. This is graphically illustrated in Figure 6.1. The three fundamental competencies are shown on the vertical dimension, and the three fundamental teaching/learning approaches are shown on the horizontal dimension. Neither of the underlying continua is shown, only the benchmarks. The resulting matrix has nine cells, one for each combination. Broken lines are used in an effort to indicate that the boundaries between these cells are not always distinct. This is our conceptual map of the territory.

Any approach or method for teaching reading that has ever been devised can be located on this map. The nine cells of the matrix define general descriptive categories for these approaches or methods. Like any large-scale map, this one should serve only a general orienting function. Not all methods are equal in scope. Some are broad and general, while others are focused and specific. Not all the cells have equal representation. Some cells have many exemplars, while others have few. We will supply a set of representative exemplars, but first we will define some of the main features of the map that demarcate the territory.

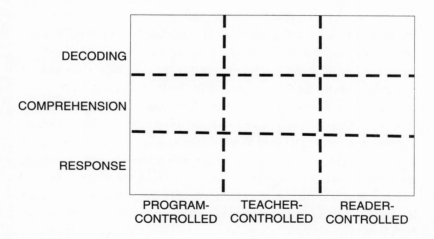

FIGURE 6.1. The matrix of nine possible combinations: a conceptual map of the territory of teaching reading.

If we draw an imaginary diagonal on Figure 6.1 from the bottom left corner to the top right corner, we bisect the map into two triangles representative of two general, opposing territories. The reader may recall our discussion of the history of these two territories from Chapters 1 and 2. In his international study of comparative reading, Downing (1973) found that, despite differences in history, culture, spoken language, or orthography, two opposite approaches to early reading could be found around the world. He called them *atomistic decoding* and *meaningful chunking*, although different sets of opposing terms have been applied and are more familiar, including *code emphasis* and *meaning emphasis* or *skills* and *whole language*. These respective oppositions are not exactly synonymous, but they do share a general theme: the distinction between teaching reading instructionally by starting with decoding and moving toward comprehension and response, and teaching reading educationally by starting with response and comprehension and moving toward decoding. We will refer to these triangles as the *skills approach* and the *holistic approach*.

The apex of the skills approach triangle is at the top left corner of Figure 6.1, program-controlled decoding. The territory expands away from that cell toward areas characterized more by comprehension and response, and by teacher and reader control. This approach is illustrated in Figure 6.2.

This teaching approach typically begins with an emphasis on a sequenced program of decoding skills instruction, gradually overlapped by a similar program of comprehension skills instruction. The skills approach has two main hallmarks: (1) both decoding and comprehension are treated as a series of skills or subskills (response is usually treated as an aspect of comprehension), and (2) instruction is primarily program-controlled in a carefully planned sequence of lessons of introduction and reinforcement. Teachers deliver the program to students with some individual variation and supplementation, and therefore some elements of teacher and reader control are typically present. The reader may recognize this approach from our discussion of the conventional basal reader ap-

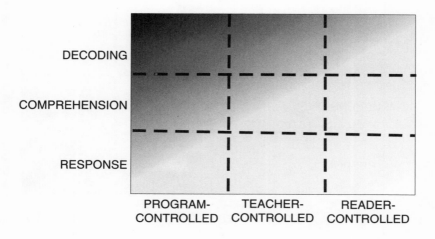

DECODING

COMPREHENSION

RESPONSE

PROGRAM-   TEACHER-   READER-
CONTROLLED   CONTROLLED   CONTROLLED

FIGURE 6.2. The general territory of the skills approach. Note that this territory is not exclusive, only that which is emphasized first.

proach in Chapter 2. Basal reader instruction is generally consistent with this description. Other more specific exemplars follow.

Conversely, the apex of the holistic approach triangle is at the bottom right corner of Figure 6.1, reader-controlled response. The territory expands away from that cell toward areas characterized more by comprehension and decoding, and more by teacher and program control. This approach is illustrated in Figure 6.3.

This teaching approach begins with emphasis on readers' own meanings and their efforts to bring those meanings to the printed page, share the meanings of others, and learn the conventions of decoding. Holistic approaches have two main hallmarks: (1) reader-centered teaching/learning in which the reader is in control of the learning situation in cooperation with the teacher, and (2) language is always used in its full communicative context, not as isolated skills (although there is less unanimity on this point). Teachers set up the learning environments in which students have some choice in the reading materials that are used in that environment, so elements of both teacher and program control are present. The reader may recognize this approach from our discussion of language experience, in-

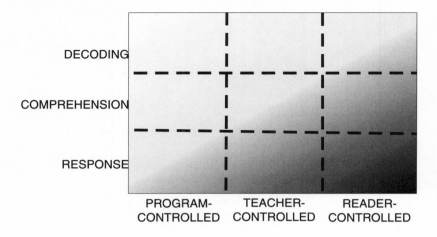

DECODING

COMPREHENSION

RESPONSE

| PROGRAM-
CONTROLLED | TEACHER-
CONTROLLED | READER-
CONTROLLED |

FIGURE 6.3. The general territory of the holistic approach. Note that this territory is not exclusive, only that which is emphasized first.

dividualized reading, and similar approaches discussed in previous chapters. We expand on these points later.

Both of these opposing approaches are viable in teaching reading. Both have long histories, prominent proponents, and ample research support. Both can be found in many different countries with different languages and cultures. However, in daily practice in schools, a blending of approaches is more common than either extreme. Such blended approaches have been referred to as *eclectic* or *balanced* approaches to teaching reading, and they take a wide variety of forms. We will refer to this approach as the *balanced approach*. No fixed formula for this approach exists, and many different combinations have been used. The common theme in balanced approaches is a judicious combination of elements from the skills approach and elements from the holistic approach.

Let us turn now to the description of some specific methods and practices that exemplify different parts of the territory. Our treatment here is meant to provide selected exemplars, not a comprehensive coverage of all possible methods and practices. That is a subject beyond the scope of this book and perhaps of any book.

Many of the exemplars used here have found research support in reviews of the published research literature (e.g., National Reading Panel, 2000).

SOME EXEMPLARS OF THE SKILLS APPROACH

Systematic Synthetic Phonics

As discussed in Chapter 4, phonics instruction is one approach to teaching decoding. Phonics instruction emphasizes the learning of letter (grapheme) and sound (phoneme) correspondences and their use in word recognition. Phonics instruction can be more synthetic (part-to-whole) or more analytic (whole-to-part), and it can be more explicitly taught or be more incidental, that is, learned indirectly with other aspects of text reading. Systematic synthetic phonics is explicit instruction in associating phonemes with graphemes and blending them to form recognizable words. Phonics generalizations governing various word sets are learned inductively, that is, by going from examples to generalizations. This sort of phonics instruction typically follows a preplanned program where letters and sounds are introduced in a specific order, although the selection, scope, and sequence of phonic units in these programs varies. In reference to Figure 6.1, this approach would be located in the program-controlled decoding cell.

A simple lesson of systematic synthetic phonics instruction might involve showing students a small set of individual letters, each on a separate large card. The teacher then pronounces a phoneme typically associated with each letter. Students pronounce the sounds after the teacher's demonstration. Practice continues until the students can produce the proper sound when each different card is shown, in stimulus–response fashion. A series of individual letters that form a word is then shown, and students blend the sounds together to form the word's pronunciation. The blending may be done slowly at first, more quickly soon after.

For example, the letters *a* and *t* might be shown on cards, and their pronunciations performed individually and then blended into the word *at*, first slowly and then more quickly. Other letters such as *c* and *b* can then be added in similar fashion to blend longer words such as *cat* and *bat* or *act* and *tab*. More letters and letter combinations are systematically added until a large number of grapheme–phoneme correspondences are well known and can be blended fluently.

Systematic synthetic phonics instruction develops out of prior instruction in alphabet knowledge and phonemic awareness and develops into whole word recognition and text reading. That is, before this approach can be productively used, students need to have some knowledge of individual graphemes and phonemes. Learning the alphabet is a common preschool activity that implicitly incorporates some phonics knowledge. For example, the names of the vowel letters *a*, *e*, *i*, *o*, and *u* are the long sounds of those vowels, and most consonant letter names incorporate phonemes typically associated with those letters (*b*, *d*, *f*, *j*, *k*, *l*, *m*, *n*, *p*, *r*, *s*, *t*, *v*, *x*, *y*, *z*). Phonemic awareness involves teaching students to recognize and manipulate phonemes in spoken syllables and spoken words without any association with graphemes or printed language. An example would be asking a student how *cat* is pronounced with the first sound removed. Combining these two funds of knowledge is involved in any form of teaching phonics, including systematic synthetic phonics. However, any form of phonics instruction is only a means to an end, not an end in itself. Phonics instruction in all forms should eventually give way to using this knowledge in whole word recognition and text reading. Programs that focus excessively on the teaching of phonics are not likely to be very effective in promoting text reading and may even be counterproductive.

A variation of systematic synthetic phonics is the use of synthetic word families or the rime-onset approach, also called the phonogram approach (Chapter 4). A word family, or phonogram, is a common vowel–consonant combination such as *-at* (a rime) that is learned as a unit. Initial consonants (onsets) are added to the rimes to synthesize words such as *bat, cat, fat, hat, mat, that, chat, flat,* and so on. There are many stable rimes and onsets in English that lend themselves to this approach. A large number of familiar words can be synthesized this way. This variation of systematic synthetic phonics is the basis of some basal reader programs that have been called "linguistic readers" or "decodable readers." It combines both phonics and some structural analysis of the syllables of simple words.

What grapheme–phoneme combinations should be taught, how many, and in what order are unanswered questions in the teaching of phonics. Consequently, programmed approaches to teaching phonics are not in universal agreement and vary in what elements are included and in what order. Certain confusions are possible in synthetic phonics instruction that need to be pointed out. For example, the pronunciation of some letters is distorted when pronounced in isolation. Take the case of the sound of *b* (*buh*), which sometimes results in mispronunciations such as *buh-at* instead of *bat*. Grapheme–phoneme correspondences can vary depending on the position of a letter in a word or syllable. The pronunciation of *a* in *am* and in *ma* is different. Other spellings are irregular or variable in their pronunciations such as *bow* (rhymes with either *cow* or *tow*) or *wind* (rhymes with either *find* or *pinned*). Most authorities feel that explicit phonics instruction should play little role after second grade unless readers are having difficulty learning phonics, whereupon a different approach might be employed in any case.

Systematic Analytic Phonics

Analytic phonics is a whole-to-part approach in which the student is first taught a number of words by sight and then taught relevant phonics generalizations and how to apply them to new words. Phonics generalizations governing sets of words are learned both inductively, going from examples to generalizations, and deductively, going from generalizations to examples. Analytic phonics can be taught more explicitly or more incidentally, that is, embedded in other aspects of text reading. In Figure 6.1, the explicit form of this approach would also be found mainly in the program-controlled decoding cell.

Systematic analytic phonics typically occurs in a series of steps: (1) learning a set of familiar sight words, (2) auditory and visual discrimination of those words and other known words, (3) word blending, and (4) application in context. A set of sight words is traditionally learned by repetition in short texts (see Figure 2.5). Auditory and visual discrimination involve hearing and seeing the similarities and differences in the letters and sounds of known words. For example, in the sentence *Bill hit the ball with a bat* a teacher might isolate and pronounce the words *Bill, ball, bat*. Students would be asked how the words sound alike, eliciting the response that they all begin with the same sound. This approach avoids some of the difficulties posed by pronouncing phonemes in isolation. Likewise, the teacher might write these words on the board and ask how they all look alike, eliciting the response that they all begin with the same letter. Students may be asked to pronounce other words they know that begin the same way. Next, the teacher would pronounce a mixed list such as *Bill, hit, ball, bat* and students would be required to discriminate the word that begins with a different sound from the rest. The students would then discriminate the written forms. Auditory and visual discrimination also could be applied to word middles or endings (e.g., *Bill, ball, bat*).

Word blending transfers phonics knowledge from studied words to new words. For example, the teacher may again draw students' attention to the words *Bill, hit, ball,* and *bat*. By interchanging the beginning letters, new words can be synthesized by analogy including *hill, hall, hat, bit*. (In this example, the analytic approach shares much with the word family or phonogram approach.) Other known words that apply to the generalizations being deduced can be added. New letters and sounds are introduced at beginning, middle, and end positions and transferred by analogy. Known and new words are also presented in new contexts to apply the phonics knowledge to text reading.

Systematic phonics, whether synthetic or analytic, has been widely used in kindergarten and first grade for many years with positive results on decoding ability. A variety of such programs have proven effective with many children of differing backgrounds. After the early grades its impact on reading comprehension is reduced, but it is still effective in many cases with children having difficulty with the decoding aspects of reading.

Repeated Readings for Fluency

Fluency can be defined as rapid, accurate word recognition that promotes clear and easy expression in reading. Fluency does not automatically guarantee comprehension, but it is regarded as a factor necessary for comprehension. It is the absence of word recognition problems that might hinder comprehension and the presence of "automaticity," the skilled recognition of words with little conscious attention to decoding them. Fluency also implies a reading rate sufficient for conversational levels of phrasing with intonation.

One popular method for developing fluency is repeated oral readings with explicit guidance and feedback from the teacher. In Figure 6.1 this technique would be centered mainly in the teacher-controlled decoding cell, with some overlap to adjacent cells, depending on the selection of materials and the amount of comprehension emphasized.

The repeated reading method is quite simple, and consists of two major components: (1) teacher modeling and (2) repeated readings by students with teacher guidance as needed. In teacher modeling, the teacher reads the text aloud to the students and the students follow along, perhaps silently at first, but joining in aloud as their confidence increases. Sometimes this is accomplished with "big books," identical, oversized demonstration versions of the children's copies. Using big books, the teacher can trace under the words and phrases being read with a finger or a pointer as the students follow along and join in. Repeated readings ensue, with the teacher providing extra assistance as needed. Here the big book is often replaced with standard-sized children's copies. Over many repeated readings, students become able to read the text independently. Criteria such as the number of words read accurately per minute can be applied, but perhaps a more reasonable goal is the achievement of conversational rate and expression. Comprehension activities and other extension activities are often included at this point.

Many variations of this approach have been developed. Dictated texts in the language experience approach can be used for repeated reading. Some variations involve recorded versions of the reading for students to use individually with headphones, but the end result must be a fluent, independent reading of the text rather than engagement in a listening activity. Teacher guidance, correction, and assessment are not available on a tape or CD. Also, many commercially available tapes are recorded at an adult reading speed, often too fast for beginners or struggling readers (Allington, 2001).

Another caution in using this technique is that children must learn to attend to word forms rather than depending on picture clues or repetitive memory. This is often accomplished by masking off all the text but a specific line or word. Guided repeated oral readings have shown a positive impact on word recognition, fluency, and comprehension across a range of grade levels and ability levels using widely available instructional materials.

Explicit Teaching of Comprehension Skills

The explicit teaching of reading comprehension assumes that (1) reading comprehension can be productively divided into subskills, and (2) those subskills can be individually taught and transferred to independent reading. Teaching separate comprehension skills is practical, but, like phonics, exactly what skills should be taught and in what order is not universally accepted. Attempts to identify and measure unique reading comprehension skills have resulted in highly correlated data, strongly suggesting that comprehension is a single underlying ability, or that it at most involves a few underlying factors. The conceptual analyses of many experts in the field also suggest that a few comprehension skills may be worth separating out for instruction. In any case, the skills approach is accomplished by the instruction of a set of comprehension skills to learn separately and later integrate. A list of such skills with some empirical and conceptual support might include:

- Word meanings
- Literal comprehension
- Inferential comprehension
- Interpreting a writer's purpose, attitude, or tone
- Following the structure of a passage

In the explicit teaching of comprehension, the teaching of these skills takes a great variety of forms. For example, passage structures take several forms such as listing, chronological order, comparison–contrast, cause–effect, or the episodic structure of stories. Examples of these may be taught separately, but their integration is the ultimate goal. Passage structures often blend and overlap. For example, causes and effects also have a chronological order because causes precede effects in time, even if the text discusses effects before their causes. A comparison–contrast structure may involve a list of points of likeness and difference. Likewise, recognizing an author's purpose or attitude involves inference in the many cases where that purpose or attitude is not literally stated.

Word meanings are often treated separately under the label *vocabulary instruction*. Teaching word meanings can be done explicitly, as in instruction in using the dictionary to locate the meanings of unknown words. However, much vocabulary is taught as a part of comprehension instruction. This typically involves selecting and preteaching key vocabulary terms from a text to be read. The key terms are often associated with each other in a way that reflects the structure of idea relationships in the text, such as its main ideas and subordinate details. For example, Chapter 4 defined *reading* using the key terms *decoding, comprehension*, and *response*. Each of those key terms was further defined using other key terms such as *literal comprehension* and *inferential comprehension*. Such vocabulary relationships can be explicitly associated in outlines or graphic organizers in vocabulary lessons that introduce a text. However, the meanings of these terms also can be derived from literal definitions supplied in the text, or from the reader's own inferences about the use of these terms in their various contexts. That is, word meanings can be gained literally or inferentially and are inherent in the structures of texts. Therefore, they are correlated with the other comprehension skills whether taught separately or not.

The second assumption of the explicit teaching of comprehension involves a specific instructional sequence that begins with teacher control and gradually moves to reader control. In Figure 6.1, this method would begin in the teacher-controlled comprehension cell (center) and gradually move toward the reader-controlled comprehension cell (center right). This instructional sequence typically includes:

- *Introduction*—the skill is defined, demonstrated through examples, and its relevance and limitations discussed by the teacher.
- *Guided practice*—students engage the skill in appropriate texts with guidance and assistance from the teacher.
- *Gradual transfer of responsibility*—the teacher initially models the skill and guides the students' efforts, but gradually releases responsibility to the students, perhaps over a series of lessons.
- *Independent application and integration*—students are given the opportunity to apply the skill in independent reading and to integrate it with other aspects of comprehension.

The explicit teaching of comprehension skills is common, practical, and has many proponents, but it also has limitations. Little evidence exists to show that the separate instruction of skills results in superior comprehension to other approaches, and no universally agreed-upon list of skills that are worth teaching exists. Teaching a combination of skills in a related way seems most effective.

Mental Imagery in Comprehension and Vocabulary Development

This method has much in common with both skills and holistic approaches, and may be seen as a bridge between them. Visualizing the events and situations described by text (i.e., mental models; see Chapter 3) is a central aspect of reading comprehension and response. Such images are constructed by readers in their own minds. Therefore, mental imagery can be seen as reader-controlled comprehension and response, more on the holistic side of Figure 6.1. However, the explicit teaching of mental imagery as a comprehension skill and a vocabulary-learning method is an established practice with an ample research record (Gambrell & Koskinen, 2002; National Reading Panel, 2000; Sadoski & Paivio, 2001). When the use of mental imagery is explicitly taught, it is more teacher- and program-controlled, on the skills side of Figure 6.1.

Two main methods of explicitly teaching students to use mental imagery have been used. In one method, students are given practice constructing images of progressively longer text units including words, sentences, paragraphs, and stories. They are sometimes shown good examples of images for the passages in the form of pictures. Bell (1991) has developed this method into a complete instructional program.

A second method is less formal and simply involves inducing imagery by telling students to "make pictures in their heads" to help them understand and remember. No specific training materials are used except concrete, imageable text passages, typically from children's literature, usually without pictures. Teachers model the process and students then try it, describing what images they formed and receiving feedback and guidance. Students are then encouraged to use this strategy in their independent reading. That is, the principles of modeling, guided practice, and independent application are applied. An interesting additional effect is that the use of mental imagery is often associated with the affective goals of more interest in reading and more enjoyment of reading.

The keyword method is a well-established method of explicit instruction in vocabulary development that involves imagery. In the keyword method, students form an interactive mental image of the definition of the new vocabulary word and a familiar, concrete word that shares a similar sound. For example, the word *potable*, meaning suitable for drinking, could be learned by using the keyword *pot* and having the learner generate an image of a pot of cool spring water waiting for someone crawling out of the desert. When later recalling the definition of *potable*, the student retrieves *pot* through its sound similarity and then recalls the image and the meaning of *potable* (Tierney, Readence, & Dishner, 1990). This method has also been successfully used in teaching foreign language vocabulary both alone and in combination with context methods (e.g., Rodriguez & Sadoski, 2000).

SOME EXEMPLARS
OF THE HOLISTIC APPROACH

Language Experience Approach

An overall exemplar of the holistic approach is the language experience approach (LEA). Chapter 5 discussed a key procedure in this approach in which children dictate sentences based on a shared experience, the teacher records their sentences on large charts, and that text is then used for repeated readings, building sight word banks, phonics learning, spelling, and other aspects of literacy. Because of its inclusiveness, it covers much of the territory darkened in Figure 6.3 and then some. Book-length explanations of the LEA are available for a more complete treatment (Allen, 1976; Stauffer, 1970). Stauffer defined this approach as an eclectic approach because it embraces a variety of practices regardless of their sources.

The essence of the LEA is that reading, writing, speaking, and listening all occur within the context of meaningful communication that emerges from the interests, abilities, and cultures of students. Allen (1968, p. 1) captured the essence of this approach for reading in a set of simple principles to be internalized by beginning readers:

- What I can think about, I can talk about.
- What I can say, I can write (or someone can write for me).
- What I can write, I can read.
- I can read what others write for me to read.

The classroom is operated as a language arts laboratory in which language skills are developed as children listen to stories, view videos or DVDs, make individual or class books, dictate stories to the teacher or each other, and study words and the alphabet. The students also record their ideas independently in spelling and writing. The classroom is typically organized into learning centers for listening, reading, writing, drama, art, research in reference works, and so on. In many ways, the LEA is a language immersion approach in which all aspects of language are studied and seen as interdependent.

The teacher works with the entire class, smaller groups, and individuals. In working with the entire class the teacher might read aloud to students, ask questions and direct discussions, or provide instruction in specific skills. In working with smaller groups, the teacher might take dictation from one student while the others observe, give specific skills instruction to groups with a common need, or complete activities initiated in the large group. In working with individuals, the teacher might suggest ideas for individual books, provide individual help with reading or writing, or listen to individual oral reading. Many other activities are possible.

The LEA can be extended into an entire curriculum covering all the language arts in various content areas. Extensions involve individualized reading (introduced in Chapter 5 and discussed later in this chapter) and reading as it occurs in different content areas such as solving word problems in math, reading maps and charts in science and social studies, conducting research using multiple sources, and so on.

Advocates point out that this approach is truly educational, deriving from student inner motivation, and that it deals with the meaningful interpretation and communication of ideas through written language from the first and extends to all aspects of reading including decoding, comprehension, and response. The evidence for the effectiveness of this broad approach is mixed, possibly because it can be applied so variously. However, it has enjoyed popularity in many countries for many years and is widely accepted in teaching reading.

Patterned Language or Predictable Books

Patterned language books, or predictable books, contain repetitive structures that allow readers to predict upcoming words, phrases, or whole episodes. Students have these books read to them, often from big books, and then they attempt to read along even though they might not be able to recognize all the words. Through repeated readings, students develop sight vocabulary by recognizing high-frequency words in dependable contexts. They also develop the ability to actively think ahead and monitor their own comprehension.

This method therefore shares much with the method described in the earlier section on repeated reading for fluency, but the goals and materials differ somewhat. The goal here is to have students develop strategies beyond fluent decoding, including the ability to use context to follow and predict an author's grammar, meanings, text structure, and story line. Therefore, the emphasis is on comprehension as well as decoding, with an increased emphasis on reader control of more aspects of reading. In Figure 6.1, the emphasis would be in the top and center cells of the right column.

The patterned language materials selected for this purpose often have some of these common characteristics:

- *Repetitive pattern.* For example, the familiar folk song "She'll Be Coming 'Round the Mountain" repeats a pattern of words in each verse.
- *Rhythm and rhyme.* The poem (song) "I Know an Old Lady Who Swallowed a Fly" uses a singsong rhythm with much rhyming and a repetitive pattern.
- *Cumulative patterns.* For example, in "I Know an Old Lady Who Swallowed a Fly" or "The House That Jack Built," each verse is carried forward and the story accumulates repetitively.
- *Picture cues.* Illustrated versions of books cue meanings and associated language. In the previous examples, pictures might cue the changing element in the pattern such as the old lady swallowing a fly, a spider, and so on.
- *Familiar sequences.* In the song "This Old Man," a sequence of numbers adds to the predictability ("This old man, he played one. . . . This old man, he played two. . . . "). Other familiar sequences are days of the week, months of the year, and so on.
- *Familiar story lines.* Well-known stories such as "The Three Little Pigs" or "The Three Billy Goats Gruff" have predictable events and even much predictable language.

Like all beginning reading approaches, this one has its strengths and limitations. Like the LEA and the method of repeated reading for fluency, it involves repeated practice with familiar material to gain confidence and skill including the development of sight vocabulary and the use of context. Patterned language books "stack the deck" in the reader's favor—they almost read themselves. However, this can also be a limitation. Some readers get so much support from the predictable context that they can "read" from memory and pay too little attention to the print. Bridge, Winograd, and Haley (1983) addressed this problem by giving students sentence strips with lines from the text to match with the book, and word cards to match with individual words. Masking pictures after initial readings may help focus attention on print as well. Bridge et al. found this approach to be significantly better than standard basal reader instruction with an emphasis on repetition both for learning sight vocabulary and for developing improved attitudes toward reading.

Invented Spelling and Writing

While writing development is not a specific topic of this book, young children's efforts to spell words as they write their own texts is a useful method for learning phonics and the conventions of print. Children's writing is part of LEA and may be done in response to reading patterned language books, among other sources. This approach involves a considerable degree of discovery as children attempt to write words whose spellings are not already known based on their alphabet knowledge and their own speech.

Developmental patterns in invented spelling have been identified that tell teachers about student growth levels. The following set of stages is abbreviated from Gillet and Temple (2000):

- *Prephonemic spelling.* Letters and letter-like forms are arranged in unbroken lines or word-like configurations with spaces between. The writing is unreadable with little or no letter–sound correspondence. This stage shows that children are aware that words are composed of groups of letters and that print is arranged in lines. This stage is characteristic of prereading and beginning reading.
- *Phonemic spelling.* Children experiment with the relationships between known letters and speech sounds. One early tendency is to spell words by their initial and/or final conso-

nants (BK = *back*). Consonant and vowel relationships emerge as students spell words by sounding them out as they spell (OSHIN = *ocean*). Letter names may be used in place of long vowels (COT = *coat*). An imperfect tendency to capture each sound with a letter is often seen, and word boundaries are not always accurate (NEOKEAKES = *New York Yankees*). This stage is characteristic of early reading.

- *Transitional spelling.* More progress is made toward conventional spelling as children progress both in reading and writing. Common spelling patterns including silent letters are represented and sometimes overgeneralized (WHALE = *whale*, WHALL = *wall*). The same word may be spelled differently in different locations. Inflectional endings are present but often spelled phonetically (PICKT = *picked*). Sentence structures are evident and some punctuation is seen (THE DAZART IS A PLAS OV BWTE. = *The desert is a place of beauty.*). Writing at this stage is largely readable by others, and children at this stage can read simple texts independently.

Eventually, conventional spelling is learned as reading and writing mature and with some direct attention to spelling. Proponents of this approach point out that children will best understand what they discover or invent themselves, and that the intricacies of phonics, sometimes difficult to teach in all their complexity, are learned more naturally this way. Invented spelling and children's writing also serves as a place to observe what children are learning about phonics and other conventions of print.

Individualized Reading and Sustained Silent Reading

Individualized reading is perhaps most appropriate beyond the very beginning reading stages. It focuses on comprehension and response, but decoding is also evaluated as part of the program. In this approach, readers are taught to take responsibility for their own reading progress, and they are surrounded with a choice of books to explore in order to promote that progress. Whole class instruction is a rarity. In Figure 6.1 it might be seen to cover the far right column, starting from the center and moving in either direction. Evaluation and skills teaching is done in student–teacher conferences that are held regularly. Individualized reading is based on three central principles adapted here from Olson (1949):

- *Self-seeking*. Readers seek out their own material from a classroom library, the school library, or other appropriate source. An ample number of appropriate children's books that are available for exploration and extended use is a requirement (5–10 per child minimum). The books should cover a wide range of interests and abilities sufficient for the class, and new titles should be added regularly.
- *Self-selection*. Readers select material primarily based on two criteria: (1) whether or not they like it and (2) whether or not they can read it. Learning to make such choices is critical to this method, although teacher direction is often needed and sometimes required. Trial and error is common.
- *Self-pacing*. Readers need time to read for extended periods without interruption in order to develop the ability to track ideas over long stretches of print and to apply their skills in their own ways and at their own pace.

Teacher–student conferences form the instructional component of this approach. Conferences are held regularly, weekly at least. They are brief, 10-minute affairs for which the student comes prepared. In a typical conference, several areas are covered: (1) checking decoding ability and fluency through the oral reading of a selected passage in the book the student is currently reading, (2) checking comprehension through question answering, retelling, summarizing, and so on; and (3) helping readers develop responses whether critical, appreciative, or applied. On the basis of these con-

112

ferences, teachers can devise needed instruction, frequently carried out in small groups of children with a similar need. This approach requires a well-read teacher who is knowledgeable about children's books, adept at the diagnosis of difficulties, and able to organize instruction and time flexibly.

A common variation of a completely individualized approach is the use of Sustained Silent Reading (SSR). In this method, a period of time is planned regularly during which students, teachers, and anyone else in the classroom puts all else aside to read something self-selected in silence and without interruption, and with no provision for conferences, quizzes, or any other form of reporting or evaluation. At lower grade levels, the interval should be daily and the time period brief, perhaps only several minutes. As grade level increases, the interval and time period increases, although SSR should occur weekly at a minimum. The teacher's role is that of a participant and model. Teachers and students alike often see SSR as an oasis in the busy day. Although SSR is not the teaching of reading per se, SSR produces achievement results comparable to other skills-based activities such as completing workbook pages. In addition, it tends to improve attitude and interest in reading with the same investment of time (Sadoski, 1984).

Student-Generated Questions

As the name implies, in this method students generate their own questions and answers about a text being read. Not one technique but several related ones, this activity was originally designed to foster active comprehension by having students inspect text more carefully and develop a questioning attitude toward reading. It was also intended to develop students who monitor their own comprehension and realize when they have failed to understand something sufficiently. In Figure 6.1, this method would be centered in the reader-controlled comprehension cell with some overlap to reader-controlled response. However, it is often introduced by teacher modeling and guided practice, so that some elements of teacher control are often present. It shares some common space with the explicit teaching of reading comprehension skills. The main difference is that in this approach questions arise from students' own comprehension monitoring rather than instruction in a specific comprehension skill.

An early and enduring method of student-generated questions is Reciprocal Questioning, or ReQuest for short (Manzo, 1968). In this technique, a predetermined segment of a text is read silently (e.g., sentence, paragraph, page) with students composing questions as they read. Students first ask their questions to the teacher and the other students, and answers are elicited. Teachers then ask questions of the students. Teachers model higher order questions that call for inference, critical reading, application, and so on. Then another segment of text is read and the procedure continues until a point when the rest of the text is read without questioning. A rule in this method is that all questions must have answers; you are responsible for answering your own question if no one else can. The shared authority in this method is often engaging to students.

An elaboration of this method called Reciprocal Teaching involves reading text segments with each student in turn (1) composing questions and answers about a segment, (2) summarizing it, (3) clarifying word meanings comprehension confusions, and (4) predicting what upcoming text may be about (Palincsar & Brown, 1984). Reciprocal Teaching has a strong record of research support (Rosenshine & Meister, 1994).

Of the different types of self-questioning strategies taught, two appear to be highly beneficial: signal words and generic questions or generic question stems. Signal words are common prompts for starting questions such as *who, what, when, where, why,* and *how.* Generic questions and generic question stems are prompts such as *What does ____ mean,* or *How does ____ cause ____,* or *What is the main idea of ____,* and so on. Teacher modeling is provided with guided practice and feedback, especially positive feedback for higher order question generation. Students sometimes are given cue cards with different signal words or prompts to aid them in composing questions. Both strategies have produced large average effects over many research studies where comprehension was tested on new material where students did not compose questions (Rosenshine, Meister, & Chapman, 1996). This finding is significant because it shows that the technique is transferred to new material. Another significant finding is that this technique is learned fairly quickly and does not require long periods of teaching to become effective.

BALANCED APPROACHES

As noted earlier, balanced approaches combine elements from both the skills approach and the holistic approach. The possible combinations are myriad and depend on the characteristics of the students, the training and dispositions of teachers, the availability of materials, and so on. The achievement of different goals and competencies at different ages with different students calls for different combinations. We discuss a balanced approach and its opportunities further in the next chapter.

FROM A MAP TO A JOURNEY

We end on a point that began this chapter. Our discussion here is a conceptual framework, a map of the territory of teaching reading rather than the territory itself. The conceptual map and the exemplars presented here are intended to organize some essential knowledge of the subject and provide a base on which to build more knowledge. The few exemplars presented here are *not* intended to be a complete review of the methods available to teachers, *nor* a review of all issues relevant to teaching reading. The actual day-to-day work of teachers and students in learning literacy is complex, and much will be learned from other sources along the journey, especially experience.

REFERENCES

Allen, R. V. (1968). *How a language-experience program works.* In E. C. Vilscek (Ed.), *A decade of innovations: Approaches to beginning reading* (pp. 1–8). Newark, DE: International Reading Association.

Allen, R. V. (1976). *Language experiences in communication.* Boston: Houghton Mifflin.

Allington, R. L. (2001). *What really matters for struggling readers: Designing research-based programs.* New York: Longman.

Bell, N. (1991). *Visualizing and verbalizing for language comprehension and thinking* (rev. ed.). San Luis Obispo, CA: Gander.

Bridge, C., Winograd, P., & Haley, D. (1983). Using predictable materials vs. preprimers to teach beginning sight words. *The Reading Teacher, 36,* 884–891.

Downing, J. (1973). *Comparative reading: Cross-national studies of behavior and process in reading and writing.* New York: Macmillan.

Gambrell, L., & Koskinen, P. S. (2002). Imagery: A strategy for enhancing comprehension. In C. C. Block & M. Pressley (Eds.), *Comprehension instruction: Research-based best practices* (pp. 305–318). New York: Guilford Press.

Gillet, J. W., & Temple, C. (2000). *Understanding reading problems* (5th ed.). New York: Longman.

Manzo, A. V. (1968). *Improving reading comprehension through reciprocal questioning.* Unpublished doctoral dissertation, Syracuse University, Syracuse, NY.

National Reading Panel. (2000). *Report of the National Reading Panel: Teaching children to read: An evidence-based assessment of the scientific research literature on reading and its implications for reading instruction.* General Report and Reports of the Subgroups. Rockville, MD: National Institute of Child Health and Human Development, U.S. Department of Education.

Olson, W. C. (1949). *Child development.* Boston: Heath.

Palincsar, A., & Brown, A. L. (1984). Reciprocal teaching of comprehension-fostering and comprehension-monitoring activities. *Cognition and Instruction, 1,* 117–175.

Rodriguez, M., & Sadoski, M. (2000). Effects of rote, context, keyword, and context keyword methods on retention of vocabulary in EFL classrooms. *Language Learning, 50,* 385–412.

Rosenshine, B., & Meister, C. (1994). Reciprocal teaching: A review of the research. *Review of Educational Research, 64,* 479–450.

Rosenshine, B., Meister, C., & Chapman, S. (1996). Teaching students to generate questions: A review of the intervention studies. *Review of Educational Research, 66,* 181–221.

Sadoski, M. (1984). SSR, accountability and effective reading instruction. *Reading Horizons, 24,* 119–123.

Sadoski, M., & Paivio, A. (2001). *Imagery and text: A dual coding theory of reading and writing.* Mahwah, NJ: Erlbaum.

Stauffer, R. G. (1970). *The language experience approach to the teaching of reading.* New York: Harper & Row.

Tierney, R. J., Readence, J. E., & Dishner, E. K. (1990). *Reading strategies and practices: A compendium* (3rd ed.). Needham Heights, MA: Allyn & Bacon.

CHAPTER 7

How?

Part III. Exemplars
of a Balanced Approach

Balanced approaches to teaching reading have recently gained much popularity and many proponents (e.g., Au, 2003; Cowen, 2003; Cunningham & Allington, 2003; Pearson & Raphael, 1999; Pressley, 2002), but the idea is not historically new (McCullough, 1968; also see Chapter 2). Moreover, the concept of "balance" has grown and changed with time. Some of what was considered appropriate in the past would be considered inappropriate today, and what is considered appropriate today may be found inappropriate tomorrow as our knowledge of reading and its teaching evolves.

This might seem to depict a hopeless situation for reading teachers: What combination is best? In this chapter, we look at the situation from the opposite perspective: the teaching of reading affords almost limitless opportunities. There is little beyond research and professional common sense to guide the chosen combinations—a balanced approach offers exciting opportunities for teacher creativity!

We begin first by advising reading teachers to become reasonably well informed about the teaching of reading by familiarizing themselves with the conceptual framework found in this book. It will serve as a structure for organizing knowledge of the many available practices and a system to variously combine and elaborate them. In reading this book, you may already have identified with the approach or combination of approaches that seems most compatible with your own views.

Next, we advise reading teachers to stay informed about current developments in the field. As in any profession, the knowledge base for teaching reading grows and changes. Current developments in theory, research, and practice provide valuable professional direction. In particular, reading teachers should place current developments in conceptual and historical perspective. Old ideas often come around in new forms expressed in currently fashionable terms.

Once reading teachers are reasonably well informed about the field, the best attitude they can adopt may be that of a spirited and imaginative inventor. Reading teachers need not invent brand-new methods and approaches every day, although there would be little wrong with their doing so. Research and established practice provide an array of rational alternatives, and practical reality usually precludes the development of a new reading curriculum in every classroom. Busy, successful reading teachers often combine and modify a selection of established, well-researched practices with creative flair.

Being inventive calls for independent thinking and decision making. Ralph Waldo Emerson once said that the scholar's first duty was self-trust; never defer to the popular cry. This may be particularly true in the teaching of reading. Polarized debates about the teaching of reading date back centuries (see Chapter 2), and recently have been called the "reading wars." While academic debates about theory and practice serve as an important forum for ideas, reading teachers might best cultivate a scholarly independence of spirit and an openness to combining ideas from different perspectives. There is no real need to take an intractable position—with experimentation and experience your own theoretical orientation will surely emerge. Fortunately, the literature about teaching reading provides a rich body of rationales for inventive experimentation.

SELECTING AND COMBINING TEACHING PRACTICES

All proponents of a balanced approach to teaching reading advocate balancing holistic education with skills instruction in various ways. However, there is no foolproof formula for a balanced approach, and no such formula is presented here. Rather, a variety of well-established, well-researched practices as described in other chapters (especially Chapter 6) are presented as possible combinatory alternatives for your consideration. Certain advantages and disadvantages are also presented for you to consider in your decisions. Experienced teachers may wish to reconsider neglected methods, and all teachers are invited to devise new, creative combinations beyond those suggested here.

The Basal Reader and the Directed Reading Activity

For centuries, a sequence of graded reading lessons in a sequence of books has been central to the teaching of reading whether it was the *New England Primer*, the McGuffey readers, or the "Dick and Jane" basals (Chapter 2). The contemporary basal reader is the current iteration of this long-established practice. Most reading teachers use a basal reader as one element in their teaching. This practice will likely continue because of the comprehensiveness of basals and state funding for basal materials.

The Directed Reading Activity (DRA) is a long-established method that is nearly synonymous with the use of the basal reader. This lesson is a "total" reading lesson that includes five steps:

- Readiness for reading
- Directed silent reading
- Comprehension check
- Oral rereading
- Follow-up skills reinforcement

The first step includes the introduction of the text, usually a story; the introduction of new and possibly problematic vocabulary; and setting a purpose for reading. The purpose for reading often involves reading to answer one or more questions or to satisfy curiosity (e.g., "Let's read to find out . . . ").

The second step involves the students reading the story silently for the purposes established as well as for any personal interests or purposes evoked. During this step, the teacher may move quietly among the students, helping any who are experiencing difficulty.

The third step involves questions and discussion to promote comprehension. The question that set the purpose for reading is a logical starting place. Questions should invoke literal and inferential comprehension and critical or applied responses. Alternatively, the story may serve as a vehicle to work on a specific comprehension skill such as inferring meanings, interpreting the author's purpose or main idea, comprehending a sequence of events or a progression of ideas, and so on.

The fourth step often occurs together with the third step by having students reread aloud segments of the text that support their answers to questions. Discussion may generate new purposes for reading or problems to be solved, and students may skim the text for appropriate passages for oral rereading to resolve issues.

The final step involves extending the development of the students' appreciation of the story or developing skills related to reading the story. Contemporary basal readers provide workbooks or activities on software to extend the appropriate skills. Skills activities are completed individually and typically involve decoding, comprehension, and response activities.

Although overreliance on the basal reader and the DRA is widely decried, the use of the basal has noteworthy advantages:

- Basals are carefully designed to deliver a controlled scope and sequence of reading skills over time that relieves the teacher from extensive planning.
- Contemporary basals are up-to-date in including attention to issues such as phonemic awareness, patterned language, children's literature selections, and so on.
- Contemporary basals promote social goals such as including a wide diversity of racial, ethnic, and cultural groups and gender roles.

Disadvantages include:

- Basal programs are heavily program- and teacher-controlled to the exclusion of reader control.
- Basals are often used with medium and large ability groups in which some students may receive insufficient individual attention or feel stigmatized by their low group status.
- Many techniques have been shown to produce better results than basals in research studies.

Supplementing the Basal Approach with Additional Comprehension and Decoding

As the name "basal" implies, these programs should best be treated as a base for teaching reading, not the whole structure. Supplementing, combining, or even superseding the basal with other approaches is therefore widely recommended and practiced. The modifications often go in two directions: more attention to decoding, or more attention to comprehension and reader response. Another common modification is to supplement the basal reader with technical or content area text by reading science, history and social studies, or mathematics. However, this hardly exhausts the possibilities of combining the basal reader and the DRA with other methods.

One possible supplement involves the use of the explicit teaching of comprehension with the basal and the DRA. The selection of a particular comprehension skill, its explanation and modeling, its guided practice over a series of lessons, and the gradual release of responsibility to the students used in the explicit teaching of comprehension skills seems to align well with the sequential lessons of the basal. This combination would call for emphasis on a particular comprehension skill across a series of consecutive basal lessons. Because many comprehension skills can be broadly applied (e.g., literal meanings, making valid inferences, summarizing, determining text structure, predicting), this combination would be practical.

However, the introduction and development of comprehension skills in the basal does not typically follow a pattern of repeating one skill at a time until some mastery level is reached. Rather, skills are introduced and then reinforced alternately so that a number of skills are being developed in parallel over time. The teacher might select from different places in the basal a set of lessons designed to emphasize a particular skill, but this would possibly violate the sequential skill development designed into the basal. Such selection could be a reasonable modification of the basal if the selected lessons were compatible in other ways, such as vocabulary difficulty, and did not assume mastery of skills not yet introduced. But using additional nonbasal text materials to teach the skill in question seems at least as practical. Supplementary text passages and skill kits can provide those materials; content area books and technical texts are also likely sources. The technical vocabulary and the variety of text characteristics found in science, social studies, mathematics, and various other subjects differ in important ways from the text typical of basals.

Student-generated questions are another logical extension of using basals and the DRA for teaching comprehension. In this technique, students compose their own questions and answers as the reading of the selection progresses. Prompts in the form of signal words and generic questions can assist students in getting started. Reading some texts in segments and practicing ReQuest or Reciprocal Teaching are useful modifications of a straight DRA.

However, some texts, such as engaging literary stories, might best be read straight through without the interruptions required for ReQuest or Reciprocal Teaching. Student-generated questions can be composed later, after the story is read through for its impact. Perhaps nonfiction, content area, and technical text might serve better for ReQuest or Reciprocal Teaching, but this is largely a matter of teacher judgment.

Supplementing the basal with additional decoding activities is also a common extension. The introduction and repetition of words or word elements such as rimes (e.g., -at) is typical of contemporary basals; decoding activities are included in basal workbooks and software programs as well. Combining the basal approach to decoding with systematic analytic phonics is a logical extension. Given a set of known words or word elements, analytic phonics activities can be applied and generalizations developed.

Attention to exceptions to the generalizations might be stressed here too. For example, the rime -ead is pronounced one way in head and bread, but a different way in bead, and alternately in read, lead, or plead, depending on grammar and meaning. Phonics analogies are another logical extension. For example, the words ending in -ead just given may have their onsets removed and combined with the rime -ow to form the rhyming set how, brow, and plow, with the exception low, and the alternative pronunciations of bow and row, depending on grammar and meaning. The analogous sets employed would depend on the words or word elements introduced in the basal and the extent of their treatment in the basal and its supplements.

Some Alternative Combinations for Early Literacy

Basals are designed to instruct readers from the very beginning, but many alternative early approaches have been shown to work just as well. Some alternatives presented here include combining in various ways the basal reader, LEA, patterned language texts, invented spelling and writing, and systematic phonics.

Holdaway (1979) suggested a three-pronged combination during the first 3 years of schooling that included graded basals, the language experience approach (LEA), and the shared-book experience with patterned language books. Each prong affords a different advantage. The basal reader provides a systematic introduction of reading skills and a gradual increase in difficulty. LEA broadly stresses immersion in all aspects of language use with more emphasis on discovery and reader control. The shared-book experience with patterned language books provides repeated readings with whole books that eventually leads to individualized reading. Decoding, comprehension, and response are differentially addressed in the three prongs, as are program-controlled teaching/learning, teacher-controlled teaching/learning, and reader-controlled teaching/learning.

This combination has broad appeal. Variants of it have been successfully used in New Zealand, Australia, Canada, and the United States (Tierney & Readence, 2000). However, as compatible as it seems, some conflicts might emerge. The planning necessary to provide a balance between the three prongs can be challenging. The sheer time and energy needed to keep track of each student's progress in each of the three prongs could be excessive. The use of a controlled-vocabulary basal is not always consistent with student-dictated language or the language used in patterned language books. However, all of these difficulties have been dealt with in practice mainly by emphasizing some parts of the combination more than others (often the basal). This combination seems to have appeal to teachers of many different theoretical persuasions.

One of the most interesting early literacy activities to emerge in recent decades is students' invented spellings and their own efforts to write. Children's efforts to write put them squarely in control in learning the conventions of printed language as well as written self-expression. Perhaps nothing that teachers or programs can do to externally impose literacy on the child can surpass children's own efforts to sort out the system for themselves. Consider the example in Figure 7.1 done by an expressive 6-year-old.

The picture shows a baseball game. Lines of spectators in the stands can be seen at the top. A batter on the left has hit a fly over the head of the pitcher and an outfielder is running back for the catch. The names of the teams are printed below in phonetic spelling: *New York Yankees* and *Baltimore Orioles*, each written as a single word. In *New York Yankees*, what appears to be a backward *S* is an *N* on its side, and the *K*'s and the final *S* are reversed. In *Baltimore Orioles*, the child ran out of room at the edge of the paper and finished the last two letters above.

FIGURE 7.1. Invented spelling of *New York Yankees* and *Baltimore Orioles* by a 6-year-old.

While this may be a charming instance of a child's self-expression, it is also an intricate example of the child's efforts to deal with phonics and spelling. Many phonemes are explicitly represented by a letter, but a few are missing. In *New York Yankees*, the /r/ phoneme in *York* is absent, as is the /n/ in *Yankees*. The /y/ phoneme at the beginning of *Yankees* is represented by an *E*, an example of letter-name spelling. That is, the sound of long *e* is phonetically similar to the /y/ sound as heard in *Yankees*. In *Baltimore Orioles*, the /r/ phonemes are likewise not represented, but an effort is made to deal with most of the *r*-controlled vowel sounds. Notice also that word divisions and top-to-bottom line order are not yet well understood. Overall, this is a fine example of the way beginners deal with the conventions of written language in early literacy efforts. Broad consensus exists among reading authorities that invented spelling is a good way to develop phonemic awareness, phonics knowledge, and a grasp of English orthography.

A plausible combination with invented spelling is synthetic phonics. In this approach to phonics, individual letter–sound matchings are taught and then synthesized into combinations and words. Consider how a synthetic phonics lesson might enhance the knowledge of the writer of the invented spelling in Figure 7.1. The phoneme /r/ is not represented at all in the writing, although it is present three times in the pronunciation of the names. Practice with the isolation of the sound of /r/ in those words and its letter association might improve both the spelling knowledge and phonics knowledge of the student. Group work for students with similar needs could be organized. Large-group lessons in certain aspects of synthetic phonics combined with writing efforts might be a productive combination.

One concern with such a combination is that some children might reduce efforts to spell words they chose in favor of using only words whose sounds and letters they have studied in their phonics lessons. They might thereby restrict their own invention and discovery. On the other hand, discovery takes time, trial, and error that teachers may wish to circumvent. Perhaps early efforts to write combined with beginning reading activities that include substantial attention to the alphabetic principle would suffice. But in some cases supplementary synthetic phonics lessons may be a reasonable and efficient way to assist progress.

Balanced Combinations for Comprehension, Appreciation, and Social Engagement

Literacy is a social activity on several levels. The communication between the author and the reader is a social act by definition, even if the particular images and meanings evoked are individual and even personal. But literacy can and should be a shared activity in a group at least part of the time. Some combinations of methods can serve well to produce group comprehension and appreciation through the diversity of responses of others.

Broad consensus exists among reading authorities that children should be read to early and often (e.g., Norton, 2003; Strickland & Morrow, 1989). This is a prime opportunity to introduce children to quality children's literature. Being read to is an essentially human activity, the literacy counterpart of the ancient tradition of storytelling. The appreciation of entertaining, moving stories provides the child with a reason to read and the motivation to get through the hard work of learning to read. And of course literary appreciation is a humanizing activity of social value in its own right. Additionally, the use of literature as the subject matter for writing has been shown to be part of an effective combination for improving written composition (Sadoski, Willson, & Norton, 1997).

Combining the reading of literature to students with instructions in mental imagery may make a positive contribution to early reading. Students can be instructed to "make pictures in their heads" while the teacher reads short passages and then describe their images to each other. Accurate examples in pictorial form might be shown to students and discriminated from inaccurate examples. Drawing pictures of images experienced and possibly using them as illustrations may also be productive. As children become proficient at creating their own inner worlds as they are read to, the teacher might forego any lessons and invite children to experience the story from the aesthetic stance of "living through" it (Rosenblatt, 1978). The use of imagery in reading should be used in both fiction and nonfiction because it produces improved comprehension, memory, and interest across genres (Gambrell & Koskinen, 2002; Sadoski & Paivio, 2001).

While reading to students can be carried into later grades, it should gradually be accompanied with, or replaced by, individualized reading and Sustained Silent Reading (SSR). A critical part of a balanced program involves providing students the opportunity to self-select reading material based on interest, difficulty, and other factors (Cunningham & Allington, 2003). Individualized reading involves assessment and instruction, whereas SSR is a time set aside for sustained encounters with books without assessment or instruction. The appropriate combination is up to the teacher, but these methods provide improvement in reading skill as well as improvements in attitudes toward reading, thereby serving affective as well as cognitive goals (Sadoski, 1984). Social sharing of books such as orally reading favorite passages is not inconsistent with these methods.

Literature Circles (Daniels, 1994; Short & Kauffman, 1995; Short, Harste, & Burke, 1996) is one currently popular activity that combines individual choice with group sharing and collaboration. The general purpose of Literature Circles is to afford students the opportunity to engage in student-led discussions of self-selected readings to socially construct the meanings of texts. The exact format of Literature Circles varies, but most descriptions of the method involve several conditions (Tierney & Readence, 2000):

- Small groups are formed for the reading of agreed-upon books. Books may be a set of the same title, a set of different titles by one author, or sets of titles with a common theme.
- Groups meet regularly to discuss the books.

- Discussions are student-led and open, intended to allow for a variety of responses and stances.
- Teachers act as facilitators and monitors, not as directors.
- Students take different roles at different times, rotating among roles such as group leader, summarizer, questioner, and content expert.
- When books are finished, new groups are formed of different students.

Limitations and drawbacks to the techniques suggested in this section on comprehension, appreciation, and social engagement are few, but they can be restrictive. Having an extensive and updated collection of children's literature is something not all classrooms can afford. Time for reading for interest and appreciation may be in short supply in an atmosphere of high-stakes testing, and the time available for reading to children, SSR, or Literature Circles might be tight in some schools. Record keeping and evaluation in these methods also poses problems because they don't lend themselves to testing. These methods are primarily teacher- and student-controlled, and they may lack the structure, scope, and sequence of more programmatic approaches such as the basal reader. Finally, there is little direct evidence at present on the effects of Literature Circles, although SSR and imagery have ample research records.

AN INVITATION

At the risk of repetition, there is no universally agreed-upon balanced approach. This situation can be seen as an invitation to invent. Like the "one best method," the best balance of methods in teaching reading is mythical. The few combinations described here are only examples using some established and/or well-researched practices that address decoding, comprehension, and response and involve varying degrees of program, teacher, and reader control. They hardly exhaust the repertoire of available methods, nor are they the most imaginative, but hopefully they convey the flavor of a balanced approach. The possibilities are profuse, and the set of combinations discussed here should only serve as a simple introduction.

The reader should not be left with the impression that this chapter is an invitation to combine practices in a pell-mell fashion without order or plan. Some potentially inconsistent combinations have been pointed out. As noted at the outset, research and informed professional judgment should guide decisions within the constraints imposed by any particular teaching situation. Real differences exist from school district to school district, from class to class, and from year to year. Moreover, professional knowledge and practice is evolving. This situation calls for flexibility within parameters established by research, experience, and practical constraints. Achieving a well-balanced approach will require a high degree of professional responsibility and vigilance. However, this is the situation in all professional fields, and it will pose no undue difficulty as long as the basic conceptual framework presented here is well understood. With this in mind, trust your own judgment and invent!

REFERENCES

Au, K. H. (2003). Balanced literacy instruction: Implications for students of diverse backgrounds. In J. Flood, D. Lapp, J. R. Squire, & J. M. Jensen (Eds.), *Handbook of research on teaching the English language arts* (pp. 955–966). Mahwah, NJ: Erlbaum.

Cowen, J. E. (2003). *A balanced approach to beginning reading instruction: A synthesis of six major U.S. research studies.* Newark, DE: International Reading Association.

Cunningham, P. M., & Allington, R. L. (2003). *Classrooms that work: They can all read and write* (3rd ed.). Boston: Allyn & Bacon.

Daniels, H. (1994). *Literature circles: Voice and choice in the student-centered classroom.* New York: Stenhouse.

Gambrell, L., & Koskinen, P. S. (2002). Imagery: A strategy for enhancing comprehension. In C. C. Block & M. Pressley (Eds.), *Comprehension instruction: Research-based best practices* (pp. 305–318). New York: Guilford Press.

Holdaway, D. (1979). *Foundations of literacy*. Sydney, Australia: Ashton-Scholastic.

McCollough, C. M. (1968). Balanced reading development. In H. M. Robinson (Ed.), *Innovation and change in reading instruction* (67th yearbook of the National Society for the Study of Education, pp. 320–356). Chicago: University of Chicago Press.

Norton, D. E. (2003). *Through the eyes of a child: An introduction to children's literature* (6th ed.). Upper Saddle River, NJ: Merrill/ Prentice-Hall.

Pearson, P. D., & Raphael, T. E. (1999). Toward a more complex view of balance in the literacy curriculum. In W. D. Hammond & T. E. Raphael (Eds.), *Early literacy instruction for the new millenium* (pp. 1–21). Grand Rapids: Michigan Reading Association and the Center for the Improvement of Early Reading Achievement.

Pressley, M. (2002). *Reading instruction that works: The case for balanced teaching* (2nd ed.). New York: Guilford Press.

Rosenblatt, L. M. (1978). *The reader, the text, the poem: The transactional theory of the literary work*. Carbondale: Southern Illinois University Press.

Sadoski, M. (1984). SSR, accountability, and effective reading instruction. *Reading Horizons, 24,* 119–123.

Sadoski, M., & Paivio, A. (2001). *Imagery and text: A dual coding theory of reading and writing*. Mahwah, NJ: Erlbaum.

Sadoski, M., Willson, V. L., & Norton, D. E. (1997). The relative contributions of research-based composition activities to writing improvement in the lower and middle grades. *Research in the Teaching of English, 31,* 120–150.

Short, K. G., & Kauffman, G. (1995). So what should I do?: The role of the teacher in literature circles. In N. L. Roser & M. G. Martinez (Eds.), *Book talk and beyond: Children and teachers respond to literature*. Newark, DE: International Reading Association.

Short, K. G., Harste, J. C., & Burke, C. (1996). *Creating classrooms for authors and inquirers*. Portsmouth, NH: Heinemann.

Strickland, D. S., & Morrow, L. M. (1989). Interactive experiences with storybook reading. *The Reading Teacher, 42,* 322–333.

Tierney, R. J., & Readence, J. E. (2000). *Reading strategies and practices: A compendium*. Boston: Allyn & Bacon.

CHAPTER 8

How Well?

The Status of Reading Achievement and Its Teaching

In this chapter we briefly consider the status of reading achievement and its teaching in the United States. There can be little doubt that a technologically advanced democracy in a global economy has need of a fairly advanced standard of literacy for its citizens. Concern has consistently been raised about the status of literacy in the United States, with claims of declining performance and declining standards in recent decades. Debates have also raged regarding the success or failure of various methods or approaches to teaching reading. How well are we actually doing?

RESEARCH ON LITERACY IN THE UNITED STATES

Literacy during much of human history was a rare commodity. The ability to read was not considered important for the lay public until

133

sometime after Johan Gutenberg's invention of the printing press (c. 1450), the rise of the middle class, and the Protestant Reformation with its emphasis on individual interpretation of the Bible. Before that time, literacy was mainly the province of the clergy and the nobility. As noted in Chapter 2, the most common books in colonial America may have been the Bible and the *New England Primer*. Direct assessment of literacy in early American schools was accomplished by oral reading.

However, the status of literacy in the United States prior to the 1970s is not well documented. Estimates of literacy in early America have been based on whether citizens could write their own name, how many years of school they had attended, or simply by whether they reported themselves to be literate or not, among other questionable means. The self-report has been used on the U.S. census to determine literacy since 1840, and the questions asked and criterion levels used have varied (Venezky, 1991). Both the quantity and the quality of national literacy well into the 20th century can only be estimated from incomplete data of questionable validity.

In a comprehensive review of the status of reading achievement in the United States commissioned by the U.S. Office of Education in 1970, Corder (1971) concluded that at that time a database did not exist to accurately determine how much of the population read well enough to meet their personal and social needs. The main problem was the absence of an agreed-upon criterion for being literate. However, after reviewing grade-equivalent scores from several standardized test publishers and extrapolating to the general public based on educational attainment, Corder estimated that of the population age 14 or older at that time, about 7% were reading below fifth-grade level and 27% were reading below eighth-grade level.

Stedman and Kaestle (1987, 1991) reviewed the status of literacy from 1880 to the 1980s. They conceptualized our knowledge of the status of literacy as having a horizontal dimension and a vertical dimension. The horizontal dimension can be defined as functional literacy, the diversity of reading tasks that occur in everyday life. The vertical dimension can be defined as academic literacy, the acquisition of literacy and subsequent grade-level achievement. The alert reader might recognize these from Chapter 3 as Goal 3: Developing the Use of Reading as a Tool to Solve Problems, and Goal 4: Developing the Fundamental Competencies of Reading at Succeedingly Higher Levels of Independence. Far less studied have been Goal 1: Developing Positive Attitudes toward Reading, and Goal 2: Developing Personal Interests and Tastes in Reading. We will return to the status of those goals later in the chapter.

Functional Literacy

Regarding the horizontal dimension, functional literacy, Stedman and Kaestle reported that total illiteracy in the United States has become quite rare, affecting only a small percentage of the people. However, they determined that a substantial proportion of the population could not read well enough to function in everyday tasks. They reviewed evidence from several sources including school attainment levels, tests of applied reading skills administered to adult population samples, comparisons of the sample population's reading level to that of commonly read materials, and a survey of job literacy requirements. They estimated that 20–30% of the adult population may have moderate to serious difficulties with common reading tasks such as reading product labels, following directions on frozen food packages, reading newspaper and magazine articles, and reading occupational manuals.

Subsequent large-scale research sharpened the estimates of Stedman and Kaestle. The 1993 National Assessment of Adult Literacy conducted by the U.S. Department of Education (Kirsch, Jungeblut, Jenkins, & Kolstad, 1993) studied the ability of the adult population over age 16 to use printed information of several kinds to function in society and achieve their own goals and potential. The study found that about 22% had only basic reading and writing skills and about 4% lacked even those. Basic ability included finding a single piece of information in a short text. Another 27% had basic literacy but were still quite limited in their ability. These people would experience considerable difficulty in performing tasks such as integrating or synthesizing information from complex or lengthy texts. Only about 4% achieved very high levels of functional literacy. A universally accepted definition of functional literacy remains elusive, but the problem certainly affects a substantial part of the population.

Academic Literacy

Regarding the vertical dimension, academic literacy, Stedman and Kaestle cautiously concluded that up until the 1970s students' reading performance in the United States at any given age probably remained stable. However, the number of students being educated in the United States during this time burgeoned due to massive population increases from waves of immigration and the postwar baby boom combined with compulsory education laws. Historically, this can be seen as holding the quality of literacy constant while greatly increasing its quantity in an increasingly diverse population, something few civilizations have ever achieved.

The single best source of data on academic literacy since the 1970s comes from the National Assessment of Educational Progress (NAEP) in reading, a national testing program initiated to coincide with the state-of-the-art report of Corder (1971). At least every 4 years since, the NAEP long-term trend assessment has been administered to large, representative national samples of children at ages 9, 13, and 17. This test is designed to be a fairly rigorous standardized test of reading comprehension, and it has changed little over time. The reading selections vary from simple narrative passages to complex articles on specialized topics. The selections include stories, essays, reports, passages from textbooks, train schedules, telephone bills, and advertisements. The test format has included multiple choice questions as well as constructed-response questions where students provide written responses. More recently, the NAEP also developed the "main" reading assessment program that is designed to reflect very current educational content and assessment methods. This test is likewise designed to be rigorous, and it is given to grades 4, 8, and 12. Different cutoff points were established in its scoring range to indicate basic, proficient, and advanced levels of reading.

Figure 8.1 shows the NAEP long-term trend scores from 1971 to 1999. Scores on all administrations of this test have been scaled to be comparable across all grades and time periods. The scale runs from 0 to 500. Several trends in this data deserve discussion. As would be expected, twelfth graders (age 17) scored higher than eighth graders (age 13) who scored higher than fourth graders (age 9). The larger increases between fourth and eighth grade than between eighth and twelfth grade are completely normal; as skill increases, gains are harder to come by. Starred scores differ to a statistically significant degree from 1999 scores for that age. As the figure shows, most scores did not differ significantly from 1971 to 1999, but where they did, the scores were higher in 1999. However, statistically significant gains do not necessarily indicate educationally significant gains. For example, the 4-point increase in average scale scores for fourth grade from 1971 to 1999 is quite small when considering the 500-point range. Overall, the trends on this long-term test from 1971 to 1999 were flat.

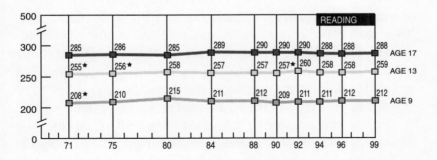

FIGURE 8.1. Trends in average scale scores for the nation at ages 9, 13, and 17 from the NAEP long-term reading assessments, 1971–1999.

NAEP "main" assessments were administered in 1992, 1994, 1998, 2000, and 2002. While not directly comparable to the NAEP long-term trend test, they are directly comparable to each other, and the latter ones can serve to suggest any growth since the last NAEP long-term assessment in 1999.

In 2000, the main assessment was administered to fourth graders only, and the average score was the same as for fourth graders in 1998. In 2002, the main assessment was administered to all three grades. The results were mixed. The average score for fourth graders increased by 2 points, the average score for eighth graders remained the same, and the average score for twelfth graders dropped by 4 points. However, only the average score for eighth graders was significantly higher than in 1992, so the trend over the decade remains flat. Taken together, there has been little change in reading achievement from 1971 until the present as determined by the NAEP tests.

However, overall averages do not tell the whole story of academic literacy. When percentages of students who reach the basic, proficient, and advanced cutoff levels are analyzed, the trend is somewhat unsettling. When averaging across the NAEP main assessments for the decade 1992–2002, 38% of the fourth graders, 28% of the eighth graders, and 24% of the twelfth graders scored *below* the basic level cutoff point. When combining the students who scored below the basic range with those who scored in the basic range, 70% of fourth graders, 69% of eighth graders, and 62% of twelfth graders scored in the basic range or below. No more than 7% of students of any age scored in the advanced range. (Keep in mind that the NAEP is a more difficult test than a minimum competency test, so a relatively small proportion of students would be expected to score at the advanced level in any case.)

Again, the trends in the NAEP reading results should be seen in historical context. During the period from 1970 to 2000 the immigrant population of the United States tripled. The number of students speaking a language other than English in the home more than doubled. And after public school enrollments declined in the

1970s and 1980s, they sharply increased again during the 1990s (Wirt et al., 2003). Therefore, a rapidly growing and increasingly diverse school population is currently being taught to read about as well as it ever was.

International Comparisons

How does the United States compare to other nations in the world? An international comparison of reading achievement in 1991 tested two age levels (Elley, 1992). Results showed that United States fourth-grade students ranked second in the world, behind only Finnish students, and ahead of the remaining 25 nations tested. On the ninth-grade level, the United States was again exceeded by Finland, was matched by 15 other nations, and was ahead of the remaining 14 nations tested. When compared only to the average score of 18 economically advanced nations who are our trading partners or competitors, about 63% of U.S. fourth graders exceeded that average and about 54% of U.S. ninth graders exceeded that average. A comparison of the content of the international test to the U.S. NAEP reading test found that the international test required mainly literal reading and simple inferences, while the NAEP test required higher levels as well (Binkley & Williams, 1996). That is, the NAEP is a more difficult test, and NAEP scores may underestimate U.S. reading achievement on an international basis.

A similar 2001 international reading assessment compared fourth graders only in 35 nations (Ogle et al., 2003). Results showed that U.S. students scored lower than students in England, the Netherlands, and Sweden; scored the same as students in eight other nations; and scored higher than students in the remaining 23 nations tested. In comparing the results from 1991 to those in 2001, no significant difference was found in the performance of U.S. students. Therefore, in comparison to many other nations, including economically advanced nations, current U.S. reading achievement appears mainly favorable and stable over time.

Attitudes and Interests

As noted earlier, far less research has been conducted on the achievement of reading goals in the affective domain. One large-scale assessment (McKenna, Kear, & Ellsworth, 1995) investigated the attitudes of a representative national sample of over 18,000 students in grades 1–6. Students responded to two rating scales comprised of items devoted to reading for recreation and reading for academic purposes. The recreational reading scale included items such as "How do you feel about spending free time reading?" The academic reading scale included items such as "How do you feel about reading your school books?" Scores on each scale ranged from 10 to 40 points. The overall attitude trends are illustrated in Figure 8.2.

The figure shows that attitudes toward reading both as a recreational pastime and as an academic pursuit begin at a relatively positive point in grade 1 and end in relative indifference in grade 6 (on the

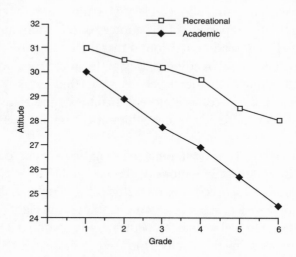

FIGURE 8.2. Trends in attitude toward recreational reading and academic reading from grade 1 to grade 6. Note that only part of the attitude scale is shown. The full scale ranges from 10 to 40, with 25 being neutral. From McKenna, Kear, and Ellsworth (1995).

10–40 scale, 25 is neutral). The researchers found that the change in attitude toward academic reading was the same regardless of student ability, gender, or ethnicity. For the change in attitude toward recreational reading, they found that attitude deteriorated more among lower ability students and boys. Another finding was that there was no meaningful relationship between student attitude and differences in use of the basal reader (heavy reliance on a basal reader, some reliance, or no reliance). Consistent with previous studies (e.g., Cloud-Silva & Sadoski, 1987), over 90% of the teachers whose classes were used in this study reported using the basal alone or a supplemented basal reader program.

The researchers concluded that one reason for the decline in attitude was the negative effect of poor reading ability as grade levels increased. That is, the cumulative impact of negative experiences with reading as students are required to read more and increasingly difficult material seems to take a continuing toll. However, other researchers have suggested that the decline may be natural because enthusiasm for all new activities declines with time (Kush & Watkins, 1996).

RESEARCH ON APPROACHES
TO THE TEACHING OF READING

Research on approaches to the teaching of reading is an extensive subject about which much has been written. Large bodies of research findings for or against different approaches have been published in respected academic journals. In keeping with our large-scale approach, we will overview broad trends in this research.

In Chapters 5 and 6 we presented a conceptual map of teaching reading that was broadly divided between the skills approach and the holistic approach. Many experimental research studies have been conducted comparing the effectiveness of these broad approaches. The results of those studies have in turn been compiled into meta-analyses (statistical summaries of studies of the same issue). Stahl and his colleagues have published two meta-analyses of the research literature comparing the skills and holistic approaches.

The first meta-analysis (Stahl & Miller, 1989) summarized the results of certain USOE first-grade studies (see Chapter 2) and 46 additional studies comparing traditional basal reader (skills) approaches with holistic approaches such as the language experience approach in the early grades. They found that 22% of the studies favored the holistic approach, 12% favored the basal reader approach, and 66% showed no significant difference. In statistically combining the effects of these studies, they found that basal reader approaches and holistic approaches were not significantly different in their effects overall. This result was found on both standardized tests and nonstandardized measures and on both measures of achievement and of attitude. Holistic approaches appeared to be somewhat better in kindergarten and in teaching word recognition, and basal reader approaches tended to be somewhat better in teaching comprehension. Higher quality studies tended to favor the basal reader approach, but differences were not large in any case.

The second meta-analysis (Stahl, McKenna, & Pagnucco, 1994) covered 45 studies conducted since 1988 in the early and middle grades. Overall, holistic approaches had a small advantage in comprehension, and skills approaches had a small advantage in decoding. Again, the holistic approach appeared to be better in kindergarten, and there were no differences on measures of attitude. Again, any differences between approaches were not large. The researchers concluded that practices drawn from both approaches appear to be effective and both are needed to meet the different needs of children in learning to read.

Studies since 1994 have produced similar results. For example, Dahl and Freppon (1995) found no substantial difference on five literacy outcome measures for skills teaching or holistic teaching in tracking students across their first 2 years of schooling. Sacks and Mergendoller (1997) studied kindergartners of different reading ability and found that lower ability children improved most in holistic classrooms, whereas all other children improved about equally under both approaches. Results of attitude measures were the same in both approaches. Overall, measurable differences between holistic approaches and skills approaches do not appear to be large. However, the research record is far from complete, and valid controversy exists on how best to investigate differences in the outcomes of these broad approaches to teaching reading (e.g., Gunderson, 1997; Pressley, 2002).

However, this does not mean that research has not revealed any useful direction for how to teach reading. Much progress in theorizing about the reading process has been made since the 1970s. Chapters 6 and 7 discussed numerous specific methods that have been researched and applied successfully enough to warrant inclusion in reading curricula. The direction at present is to try to find the best combination of methods for particular groups of children. Many educators in reading have suggested balancing elements of different approaches to achieve the most progress in decoding, comprehension, and response. A consensus may be emerging that reading occurs in stages of development where different approaches may be more appropriate at the different stages (e.g., Chall, 1996). However, exactly what the stages are and what methods may be best for a given stage are not widely accepted as yet.

SOME FINAL CONCLUSIONS
AND SPECULATIONS

The status of reading achievement in the United States can easily be seen as a glass half full or a glass half empty. There is reason to conclude that overall literacy levels in the United States have remained stable or increased during the last century or more. This conclusion should be seen in the context of *more* educational opportunity for *more* students of *more* diversity during that time. Contrary to some opinion, there is no hard evidence that we are in the midst of a dramatic decline in national reading achievement. Students in the United States consistently perform as well or better than students in previous generations and in all but a few other nations.

However, in both functional literacy and academic literacy, large percentages of the population perform at low levels and only small percentages perform at advanced levels. To many, this situation is unacceptable in a technologically advanced democracy in a global economy. Even if literacy achievement in the United States today is the equal or better of what it ever was, the demand for literacy at higher levels appears to be increasing. After a historical examination of selected European and U.S. models of teaching literacy, Resnick and Resnick (1977) concluded that reading instruction has been aimed at attaining either a low level of literacy for a large number of people or a high level of literacy for an elite few. The contemporary goal of high levels of literacy for an entire population is a relatively recent historical development that poses a challenge not previously faced.

This is an appropriate point to revisit the goals of teaching reading elaborated in Chapter 3 and discussed earlier in this chapter. The evidence reviewed earlier indicates continued success in meeting the goals in the cognitive domain with the qualification that advanced levels of comprehension and response are attained by relatively few in either functional reading or academic reading. Basic literacy is achieved or surpassed by a large majority of the population, but many citizens still struggle with daily reading tasks at work or at school. The goals in the affective domain have been less well met. Elementary school children start out with a moderately positive attitude toward reading, but that attitude slides to indifference by grade six, suggesting a trend toward aliteracy. Taken together, the largest problem in teaching reading may be how to motivate students to higher levels of achievement. This is a more challenging problem than might be assumed because it is somewhat a matter of national values.

From his comprehensive review of the status of reading achievement and its teaching at that time, Corder (1971, pp. 143–144) concluded:

> All methods of reading instruction instruct some children (probably the same ones) well and do not succeed with some small portion of others that have been studied.

The national reading problem is not that massive numbers of students cannot read in the sense of not knowing the grapheme–phoneme correspondences but in the fact that many persons do not wish to read for pleasure or information and do not comprehend either written or oral messages well.

In effect, the national reading problem might as easily be called the national thinking or comprehension problem and the schools are only minutely responsible for the fact that massive numbers of our citizens are, essentially, not inclined to develop or maintain reading and comprehension skills necessary for their own self selected goals and life space.

While progress has been made in identifying successful methods of teaching reading since then, one is tempted to say that the picture has not fundamentally changed. Whether the schools can motivate the population to higher levels of literate comprehension is questionable. This perspective is not the one usually adopted by policymakers.

After the first four NAEP long-term reading reports, Carroll (1987) summarized the results that far and determined that it might be unrealistic to expect any *major* improvements over present levels of literacy. While he felt that some further progress might be made toward improving the reading of students at lower levels of achievement through improved teaching and more practice, progress at the upper levels of achievement would be difficult to attain for several reasons. One reason is that progress at high levels calls for teaching higher order reading skills. Exactly what these skills are, and how best to teach them, has not been completely spelled out. Also, reaching high levels of reading calls for increasingly wide and deep vocabulary, better ability to understand complex sentences and texts, and substantial background knowledge of the world. Carroll (1987, p. 429) felt that these tasks are somewhat similar to what is traditionally considered verbal intelligence or scholastic aptitude:

The degree to which reading ability can be improved beyond a level of functional literacy is in part a matter of the degree to

145

which verbal intelligence can be increased. The research literature on this question does not yet give any large measure of hope . . . for the most part, we must confront the possibility that somehow the nation will have to accommodate itself pretty much to the levels of reading skill now attained by various segments of the population.

However, Carroll's speculation may be too pessimistic. Progress in teaching reading will clearly continue, and it is also clear that higher level reading skills can be improved for both children and adults of normal ability through increased time and effort using existing methods. The question is perhaps not one of means but of motivation. We have the means to improve, but do we have the motivation? To what level of literacy does the public aspire?

Whether forces such as legislation, the economy, social equity, or national security can motivate the public aspiration to a much higher level of literacy remains to be seen. But we have the means to produce advanced levels of reading and to reduce reading failure. Of the different approaches to teaching reading that have been so far developed, none appears to be the "best," but many ways produce very successful results. Further advances in reading theory, research, technology, and application may brighten the future considerably. This future will certainly hold interesting developments for the teacher of reading. There has perhaps never been a more challenging and exciting time.

REFERENCES

Binkley, M., & Williams, T. (1996). *Reading literacy in the United States: Findings from the IEA Reading Literacy Study.* Washington, DC: National Center for Educational Statistics, U.S. Department of Education.

Carroll, J. B. (1987). The national assessments in reading: Are we misreading the findings? *Phi Delta Kappan, 68,* 424–430.

Chall, J. S. (1996). *Stages of reading development* (2nd ed.). Fort Worth, TX: Harcourt Brace College Publishers.

Cloud-Silva, C., & Sadoski, M. (1987). Reading teachers' attitudes toward basal reader use and state adoption policies. *Journal of Educational Research, 81,* 5–16.

Corder, R. (1971). *The information base for reading: A critical review of the information base for current assumptions regarding the status of instruction and achievement in the United States.* Educational Testing Service, U.S. Office of Education Project 0-9031, Final Report. (ERIC Document Reproduction Service No. ED 054 922)

Dahl, K. L., & Freppon, P. A. (1995). A comparison of innercity children's interpretations of reading and writing instruction in the early grades in skills-based and whole language classrooms. *Reading Research Quarterly, 30,* 50–74.

Elley, W. B. (1992). *How in the world do students read?* The Hague, The Netherlands: International Association for the Evaluation of Educational Achievement.

Gunderson, L. (1997). Whole-language approaches to reading and writing. In S. A. Stahl & D. A. Hayes (Eds.), *Instructional models in reading* (pp. 221–247). Mahwah, NJ: Erlbaum.

Kirsch, I. S., Jungeblut, A., Jenkins, L., & Kolstad, A. (1993). *Adult literacy in America: A first look at the findings of the National Adult Literacy Survey.* Washington, DC: National Center for Educational Statistics, U.S. Department of Education.

Kush, J. C., & Watkins, M. W. (1996). Long-term stability of children's attitudes toward reading. *Journal of Educational Research, 89,* 315–319.

McKenna, M. C., Kear, D. J., & Ellsworth, R. A. (1995). Children's attitudes toward reading: A national survey. *Reading Research Quarterly, 30,* 934–956.

Ogle, L., Sen, A., Pahlke, E., Jocelyn, L., Kastberg, D., Roey, S., & Williams, T. (2003). *International comparisons in fourth-grade reading literacy: Findings from the Progress in International Reading Literacy Study (PIRLS) of 2001.* Washington, DC: National Center for Educational Statistics, U.S. Department of Education.

Pressley, M. (2002). Effective beginning reading instruction. *Journal of Literacy Research, 34,* 165–188.

Resnick, D. P., & Resnick, L. B. (1977). The nature of literacy: An historical exploration. *Harvard Educational Review, 47,* 370–385.

Sacks, C. H., & Mergendoller, J. R. (1997). The relationship between teachers' theoretical orientation toward reading and student outcomes in kindergarten children with different initial reading abilities. *American Educational Research Journal, 34,* 721–739.

Stahl, S. A., McKenna, M. C., & Pagnucco, J. R. (1994). The effects of whole-language instruction: An update and reappraisal. *Educational Psychologist, 29,* 175–185.

Stahl, S. A., & Miller, P. D. (1989). Whole language and language experience approaches for beginning reading: A quantitative research synthesis. *Review of Educational Research, 59,* 87–116.

Stedman, L. C., & Kaestle, C. F. (1987). Literacy and reading performance in the United States, from 1880 to the present. *Reading Research Quarterly, 22,* 8–46.

Stedman, L. C., & Kaestle C. F. (1991). Literacy and reading performance in the United States from 1880 to the present. In C. F. Kaestle, H. D. Moore, L. C. Stedman, K. Tinsley, & W. V. Tollinger, *Literacy in the United States: Readers and reading since 1880* (pp. 75–128). New Haven, CT: Yale University Press.

Venezky, R. (1991). The development of literacy in the industrialized nations of the West. In R. Barr, M. L. Kamil, P. B. Mosenthal, & P. D. Pearson (Eds.), *Handbook of reading research* (Vol. 2, pp. 46–67). White Plains, NY: Longman.

Wirt, J., Choy, S., Provasnik, S., Rooney, P., Sen, A., & Tobin, R. (2003). *Condition of education 2003.* Washington, DC: National Center for Educational Statistics, U.S. Department of Education.

Author Index

Subject Index

Literature, 25, 27, 128–130
Literature Circles, 129–130
Look–say approach, 32

M

McGuffey readers, 22–24
Meaning emphasis approach,
    6, 36, 94
Mental imagery, 25, 105–106,
    128–129
Modified alphabet, 36
Morphemes, 63–64

N

National Assessment of
    Adult Literacy, 135–138
National Assessment of
    Educational Progress
    (NAEP), 136–139, 144
National Reading Panel, 97, 105
New England Primer, 18–19

O

Oral reading emphasis, 15, 20, 27
Orbis Sensualium Pictus, 16–18,
    25, 26, 32

P

Patterned language, 108–110,
    125

Phoneme, defined, 61
Phonemic awareness, 40, 98
Phonics, 22, 35, 61–62
    analytic, 18, 62,
        99–101, 124
    synthetic, 16, 20, 25, 62,
        97–99, 127
Programmed reading, 36

R

Reading achievement in the
    United States, 133 ff.
Reasons for reading, 46–47
Response, 71–75

S

Sentence method, 25
Sight vocabulary,
    31–32, 64–65
Silent reading emphasis,
    25, 29
Skills approach, 94,
    141–143
Skills management programs,
    36, 82–83
Social engagement,
    128–130
Stages of reading, 53–54
Standardized tests, 28, 90,
    136–139, 142
Story method, 27
Structural analysis, 62–64
Student-generated questions,
    113–115, 124